D1551362

WITHDRAWN

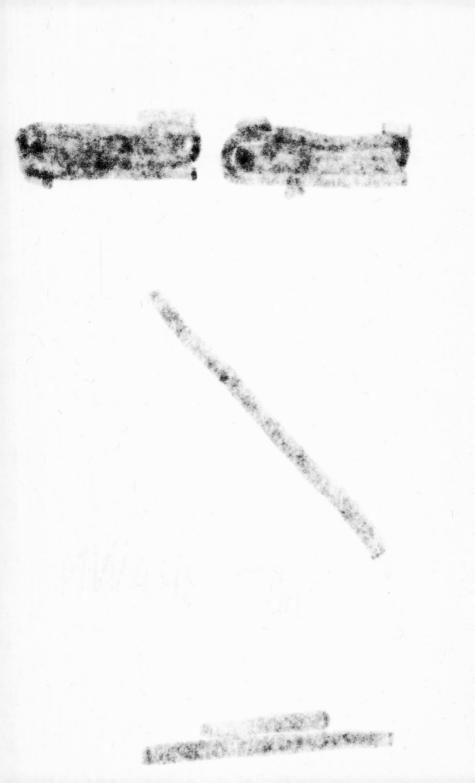

The Scarecrow Author Bibliographies

IRIS MURDOCH
and
MURIEL SPARK:
A Bibliography

by
Thomas T. Tominaga
and
Wilma Schneidermeyer

The Scarecrow Author Bibliographies, No. 27

The Scarecrow Press, Inc.
Metuchen, N.J.   1976

A
012
T657i
1976

Library of Congress Cataloging in Publication Data

Tominaga, Thomas T
    Iris Murdoch and Muriel Spark: a bibliography.

    (The Scarecrow author bibliographies; no. 27)
    Includes indexes.
    1. Murdoch, Iris--Bibliography. 2. Spark, Muriel--
Bibliography. I. Schneidermeyer, Wilma, joint author.
Z8606.3.T65   [PR6063.U7]   016.82'09'00914   76-909
ISBN 0-8108-0907-9

CONTENTS

iii

FOREWORD

This bibliography of Iris Murdoch and Muriel Spark is our attempt to bring together all their writings, and the accompanying criticism and translations, from the beginning of their careers to 1975. Their books are so widely translated and reviewed throughout the world that no bibliography can include every entry at this time. Nevertheless, our intention is comprehensiveness; no entry has been purposely omitted.

The organization is alphabetical throughout, with the entries numbered consecutively. Numbers in the index refer to individual entries, not to manuscript pages. To accommodate particular interests, the chronologies which precede the Introduction include biographical information and listings of the major works. Because many critics combine the purposes of review and assessment when writing about modern literature, we have adopted the following plan: any secondary work published in a periodical that we could establish as having both a title and an author is listed under the heading Critical Essays. Material enclosed in brackets following many such entries is either a cross-reference to primary works discussed or an annotation made because it seemed to us to be helpful. Entries without titles appear in the lists of reviews which follow publication data and translations of each book. Exceptions to this plan occur only when the content of an anonymous entry dictates its being listed as a critical essay. For the most part, however, assignment of an entry to the category of Critical Essays or Reviews is arbitrarily made regardless of length or content, and is not meant to imply the importance of titled over untitled entries.

Some bibliographies and checklists we found helpful in compiling this one. Special mention should go to Laraine Civin's 1968 bibliography of Murdoch and to Bernard Stone's checklist of Muriel Spark's work in Derek Stanford's <u>Muriel Spark</u>, published in 1963, although, by his own admission, Stone left much to future bibliographers.

We hope that this bibliography will be helpful to critics of contemporary literature generally. Particularly we hope it will stimulate studies in philosophy, religion, and comparative literature, because both writers offer much to the interdisciplinary scholar.

SOURCES

Abstracts of English Studies
American Book Publishing Record
Annual Bibliography of English Language and Literature
Biblio [catalog of works published in French]
Bibliografía Española
Bibliografia Nazionale Italiana
Bibliographic Index
Bibliographie de la France
Bibliographie de la Philosophie [Bibliography of Philosophy]
Bibliography of Philosophy [Bibliographie de la Philosophie]
Bibliothèque Nationale
Biography Index
Book Review Digest
Book Review Index
Books in Print [books published in the United States]
British Books in Print
British Humanities Index
British Museum General Catalogue of Printed Books
The British National Bibliography
British Union-Catalogue of Periodicals
Bulletin of Bibliography and Magazine Notes
Canadian Books in Print
Canadian Index
Catalogo dei Libri Italiani in Commercio
Catalogue de l'Edition Française [French books in print]

Catholic Periodical and Literature Index

Chicorel Theater Index to Plays

Cumulative Book Index

Current Biography

Deutsche Bibliographie

Dissertation Abstracts [now called Dissertation Abstracts International]

Essay and General Literature Index

Fiction Catalog

Index to Book Reviews in the Humanities

Index to Plays in Periodicals

Index to Religious Periodical Literature

Index Translationum [international bibliography of translated works]

International Index [now called Social Sciences and Humanities Index]

International Who's Who

Internationale Bibliographie der Rezensionen [international bibliography of book reviews of scholarly literature]

Italia Bibliographica

Library of Congress Author Catalog

Libri e Rivista D'Italia

Libros en Venta [catalog of works published in Spanish]

Libros Españoles

Literatur Katalog

Les Livres de l'Année--Biblio

MLA International Bibliography [PMLA]

The National Union Catalog

New York Times Index

Newspaper Index, 1972-- [Chicago Tribune, Los Angeles Times, The New Orleans Times-Picayune, The Washington Post]

Newspapers in Microform: Foreign Countries 1948-1972

Newspapers in Microform: United States 1948-1972

1974 Ayer Directory of Publications: Newspapers and Magazines

Ottemiller's Index to Plays in Collections (5th ed.)

Paperbound Books in Print

Philosopher's Index

Play Index

Readers' Guide to Periodical Literature

Répertoire Bibliographique de la Philosophie

Short Story Index

Social Sciences and Humanities Index [formerly International Index]

The Times Index [London]

Union List of Serials in the Libraries of the United States and Canada

Verzeichnis Lieferbarer Bücher

Whitaker's Cumulative Book List

A World Bibliography of Bibliographies

The Year's Work in English Studies

The Year's Work in Modern Language Studies

CHRONOLOGY: (JEAN) IRIS MURDOCH

Biography and Chronology of Major Publications

1919:   Born on July 15 in Dublin, Ireland of Anglo-Irish parents, Wills John Hughes and Irene Alice (Richardson) Murdoch

1937:   Completed secondary education, which was begun at Froebel Educational Institute, London, and finished at Badminton School, Bristol

1938-42: Studied at Sommerville College, Oxford University

1942:   Received B. A. degree with first class honors in Classical Moderations and Greats

1942-44: Assistant Principal in the British Treasury, London

1944-46: Administrative Officer with the United Nations Relief and Rehabilitation Administration in London, Belgium, and Austria

1947-48: Sarah Smithson Studentship in Philosophy at Newnham College, Cambridge University

1948:   Appointed Fellow of St. Anne's College, Oxford

1948-63: Served as University Lecturer in Philosophy, St. Anne's College, Oxford

1951:   "Thinking and Language"

1952:   "Nostalgia for the Particular"

1953:   Sartre: Romantic Rationalist

1954:   Under the Net

1956:   The Flight from the Enchanter
           Married John Oliver Bayley, a novelist, poet, and
           critic
           "Vision and Choice in Morality"

1957:   "Metaphysics and Ethics"
           The Sandcastle

1958:   The Bell
           "A House of Theory"

1959:   Lecturer at Yale University
           "The Sublime and the Beautiful Revisited"
           "The Sublime and the Good"

1961:   A Severed Head

1962:   An Unofficial Rose

1963:   "Freedom and Knowledge"
           Named Honorary Fellow, St. Anne's College, Ox-
           ford
           The Unicorn

1963-67:   Lecturer at Royal College of Art, London

1964:   The Italian Girl

1965:   The Red and the Green

1966:   The Time of the Angels

1967:   The Sovereignty of Good over Other Concepts

1968:   The Nice and the Good

1969:   Bruno's Dream

1970:   A Fairly Honourable Defeat
           The Servants and the Snow
           The Sovereignty of Good

1971:   An Accidental Man

1972:   The Three Arrows

CHRONOLOGY: MURIEL (SARAH) SPARK

Biography and Chronology of Major Publications

1918:   Born in Edinburgh, Scotland of a Jewish father
            and Scottish mother, Bernard and Sarah Eliza-
            beth (Uezzell) Camberg

1936:   Completed education at James Gillespie's School
            for Girls, Edinburgh

1937:   Left Edinburgh to live in Africa (Rhodesia and
            South Africa)
            Married S. O. Spark (engineer)

1938:   Marriage was dissolved

1944:   Returned to war-time England from Africa

1944-46:   Worked in the Political Intelligence Department of
            the British Foreign Office
            Employed as a staff member of the trade maga-
            zine Argentor (London)

1947-49:   General Secretary of the Poetry Society, London
            Editor of The Poetry Review (London)

1949:   Introduced a new journal, Forum Stories and
            Poems, of which only issues No. 1 and 2 of Vol-
            ume I were published

1950:   Tribute to Wordsworth

1951:   Child of Light: A Reassessment of Mary Woll-
            stonecraft Shelley
            Recipient of The Observer Story Prize for the
            winning short Christmas story, "The Seraph and
            the Zambesi"

1952:	The Fanfarlo and Other Verse
	Selected Poems of Emily Brontë (also titled as A Selection of Poems by Emily Brontë)
1953:	Emily Brontë: Her Life and Work
	John Masefield
	My Best Mary: Selected Letters of Mary Shelley
1954:	The Brontë Letters (also titled as The Letters of the Brontës)
	Conversion to Roman Catholicism
1957:	The Comforters
	Letters of John Henry Newman
1958:	The Go-Away Bird and Other Stories
	Memento Mori
	Robinson
1960:	The Bachelors
	The Ballad of Peckham Rye
1961:	The Prime of Miss Jean Brodie
	Voices at Play
	Visited Jerusalem during the trial of Adolf Eichmann, to gather material for The Mandelbaum Gate
1962:	Recipient of the Italia Prize for radio drama based on The Ballad of Peckham Rye
1963:	Doctors of Philosophy
	The Girls of Slender Means
	Named Fellow of the Royal Society of Literature
1964:	Moved from London to New York, where she lived about 10 months of the year in an apartment near the United Nations building
1965:	The Mandelbaum Gate
	Recipient of the James Tait Black Memorial Prize for Fiction for The Mandelbaum Gate
1967:	Collected Poems I
	Collected Stories I
	Appointed Officer, Order of the British Empire
	Moved from New York to Rome, Italy, where she has made her home

INTRODUCTION

Our reasons for compiling this bibliography of Iris Murdoch and Muriel Spark are threefold. First, although there are some brief bibliographies and checklists available, they are not up to date, nor do they provide extensive reviews, translations, or foreign criticism. Second--and this was our original attraction--we chose to treat these writers in a single bibliography because they provide the kind of reasoned discussion within and across several disciplines of which we approve. As the Dissertations sections alone of this bibliography show, both invite readers from diverse fields to re-examine the relationship of literature, philosophy, psychology, sociology, and religion. And third, we consider Murdoch and Spark to be intellectual and philosophical writers in the best sense of these words, and thus worthy of the critical attention of scholars concerned with writers who are saying something about the crisis of our times. To support the third consideration, we wish to outline briefly some similarities between Murdoch and Spark--but first a word of qualification.

Both Iris Murdoch and Muriel Spark are contemporary British novelists who have earned abundant critical praise while achieving popular success. When we combine them into a joint bibliography we do not mean to suggest to the reader unfamiliar with their work that there stand waiting to be discovered whole scores of unnoticed affinities, although possibly this is the case, as it may be with contemporary writers generally. We wish to acknowledge from the beginning that each has long ago earned separate critical appraisal. Since the early 1950s both have written diligently and consistently, turning out on the average an important book every year, as is clear from our chronological listings of their publications.

Our third reason for this bibliography is consideration of Murdoch and Spark as philosophical writers. They see the novel as a vehicle for examining a moral question, particularly

as a way of challenging deeply fixed world views. They are
considered moralists on at least two levels. They attempt to
redefine reality and truth for a generation of people who can
no longer believe in liberal humanistic or traditional Christian doctrine.   Beyond that, there is for both an alternative
world view which they wish to present for serious study; this
new view is in the tradition of Camus and Sartre in some
respects, although neither is a thoroughgoing existentialist.
Life in its contingency--life lived in acknowledgment of the
absurd, the ridiculous, the mundane--is the subject of most
of their novels.   In the worlds of Murdoch and Spark there
are no easy antidotes for pain.   Simple human sympathy is
not enough to relieve the present condition, nor can it provide
lasting satisfaction or inner joy.   But it does count for something.   Murdoch and Spark have set about to reassess its
meaning and value.

     Not only moral positions, but artistic assumptions as
well fall under their scrutiny, as both work self-consciously
as novelists; which is to say that they concern themselves
with questions of aesthetic philosophy both in their fiction
and in public addresses, interviews, and formal essays.   For
both, the novel itself offers a medium for pronouncement on
aesthetic questions, and Murdoch and Spark's definitions of
the artist's task are in contrast to present orthodoxy.   Thus,
perhaps, they invite also the attention of aestheticians, for
both work against Aristotelian assumptions, preferring to hold
with the Platonic vision of the Good.

                                         T. T. T.

                                         W. S.

                              2

PART I

WRITINGS BY
IRIS MURDOCH
(to 1975)

A. NOVELS

1. An Accidental Man. Harmondsworth, Middlesex, England: Penguin Books, Ltd., 1973, paperback. London: Chatto & Windus, Ltd., 1st ed., 1971. New York: Viking Press, 1971, 1972 and Warner Paperback Library, 1973, 1974, paperback.

   Reviews of An Accidental Man

   2. Anonymous. Booklist 68 (1 March 1972):550.

   3. _____. British Book News [no number] (January 1972):83-84.

   4. _____. New Yorker 47 (12 February 1972): 102-103.

   5. _____. Virginia Quarterly Review 48 (Summer 1972):c.

   6. Avant, John A. Library Journal 97 (15 January 1972):215.

   7. Cooke, Michael. Yale Review 61 (June 1972):559.

   8. Degnan, James P. Hudson Review 25 (Summer 1972):330-37.

   9. Hill, W. B. America 126 (20 May 1972):549.

   10. Kennedy, Eileen. Best Sellers 31 (1 March 1972): 530.

   11. Lemon, Lee T. Prairie Schooner 46 (Fall 1972): 266-67.

   12. Mallet, Gina. Saturday Review 55 (29 January 1972):68.

4

13. Meades, Jonathan. Books and Bookmen 17 (January 1972):37.

14. Wade, Rosalind. Contemporary Review 220 (January 1972):46-47.

15. The Bell. Harmondsworth, Middlesex, England: Penguin Books, Ltd. , 1969, paperback.
London: Chatto & Windus, Ltd. , 1st ed. , 1958, 1959.
New York: Viking Press, 1958 and Avon Books, Bard edition, 1966, 1974, paperback.
Toronto: Clarke, Irwin & Company, Ltd. , 1958.

Translations of The Bell

16. Murdoch, Iris. La Campana. [No trans. given.] Santiago, Chile: Editorial Pomaire, n. d.

17. _____. Dzwon. Trans. by Krystyna Tarnowska. Warsaw: Państwowy Instytut Wydawniczy, 1972.

18. _____. Les Eaux du Péché. Trans. by Jérôme Desseine. Paris: Librairie Plon, 1958, 1961.

19. _____. Kane. Trans. by Maruya Saiichi. Tokyo: Shûeisha, n. d. [ca. 1968].

20. _____. De Klok. Trans. by Hella Haase. Amsterdam: Uitgeverij Contact N. V. , 1962, 1970 and Antwerpen: Contact, 1965.

21. _____. Klokken. Trans. by Inger-Sophie Manthey. Oslo: Gyldendal Norsk Forlag, 1966.

22. _____. Klokken. Trans. by Michael Tejn. Copenhagen: Schønbergske Forlag, 1966.

23. _____. O Sino. Trans. by A. Neves-Pedro. Lisbon: Portugália Editora, 1965.

24. _____. Die Wasser der Sünde. Trans. by Maria Wolff. Zürich: Neue Schweizer Bibliothek, 1970.

Reviews of The Bell

25. Anonymous. Best Masterplots, 1954-1962. Ed.

by Frank N. Magill. New York: Salem Press,
1963, pp. 35-37.
Also in Survey of Contemporary Literature, vol.
1. Ed. by Frank N. Magill. New York: Salem
Press, 1971, pp. 362-64.

26. _____. Booklist 55 (1 October 1958):58

27. _____. Booklist 55 (1 November 1958):127.

28. _____. Bookmark [New York State Library,
Albany] 18 (November 1958):38.

29. _____. British Book News no. 221 (January
1959):73.

30. _____. British Book News no. 260 (April
1962):306.

31. _____. Kirkus Reviews 26 (15 August 1958):
618.

32. _____. Masterplots Comprehensive Library
Edition, vol. 1. Ed. by Frank N. Magill. New
York: Salem Press, 1968, pp. 377-79.

33. _____. Masterplots 1959 Annual. Ed. by
Frank N. Magill. New York: Salem Press,
1959, pp. 23-26.

34. _____. New Yorker 34 (22 November 1958):
221.

35. _____. Saturday Review 49 (24 September
1966):40.

36. Bannon, Barbara A. Publishers Weekly 189
(June 1966):129.

37. Price, Martin. Yale Review 48 (December 1958):
272.

38. Rees, Goronwy. Listener 60 (18 December 1958):
1046.

39. Rolo, Charles. Atlantic Monthly 202 (November
1958):173-74.

40.   Wood, Frederick T. _English Studies_ 41 (1960):
      50-51.

41.   _The Black Prince._ London: Chatto & Windus, Ltd.,
      1st ed., 1973.
      New York: Viking Press, 1973.

Reviews of _The Black Prince_

42.   Anonymous. _Booklist_ 69 (15 July 1973):1050.

43.   _____. _British Book News_ [no number] (June
      1973):413.

44.   _____. _Choice_ 10 (September 1973):981.

45.   _____. Clarke, Irwin & Company, Ltd.,
      Toronto, Publication Listing (Spring and Summer
      1973):27.

46.   _____. _Kirkus Reviews_ 41 (15 March 1973):
      339-40.

47.   _____. _New York Times Book Review,_ 10
      June 1973, p. 39.

48.   _____. _New York Times Book Review,_ 2 De-
      cember 1973, p. 76.

49.   _____. _New York Times Book Review,_ 11
      August 1974, p. 20.

50.   _____. _Observer_ [London], 2 March 1975,
      p. 23.

51.   _____. _Psychology Today_ 7 (October 1973):
      140.

52.   _____. _Publishers Weekly_ 203 (16 April
      1973):48.

53.   _____. _Virginia Quarterly Review_ 49 (Autumn
      1973):R136.

54.   _____. _Vogue_ 161 (May 1973):148-49, 194-95.
      [Editor's Note and an excerpt from _The Black
      Prince._]

8   Iris Murdoch

55. Annan, Gabriele. Listener 89 (22 February 1973):
     249-50.

 56. Avant, John A. Library Journal 98 (1 June 1973):
     1844.

 57. Brockway, James. Books and Bookmen 18 (April
     1973):29-30.

 58. Bromwich, David. Commentary 56 (September
     1973):88-89.

 59. Broyard, Anatole. New York Times, 6 June
     1973, p. 45

 60. De Feo, Ronald. Hudson Review 26 (Winter
     1973-74):784-85.

 61. Gordon, Jan B. Commonweal 99 (14 December
     1973):300-302.

 62. Goshgarian, Gary. Christian Science Monitor,
     27 June 1973, p. 9.

 63. Hill, W. B. America 129 (17 November 1973):
     382.

 64. Lindroth, James R. America 129 (1 September
     1973:130-31.

 65. Phillipson, J. S. Best Sellers 33 (15 June 1973):
     140.

 66. Price, Martin. Yale Review 63 (October 1973):
     80.

 67. Weeks, Edward. Atlantic Monthly 232 (July
     1973):101-102.

 68. Bruno's Dream. Harmondsworth, Middlesex, England:
     Penguin Books, Ltd., 1970, paperback.
     London: Chatto & Windus, Ltd., 1st ed., 1969.
     New York: Viking Press, 1969 and Dell Publishing
     Company, Inc., 1969, paperback.

          Translations of Bruno's Dream

 69. Murdoch, Iris. Bruno No Yume. Trans. by

Nakagawa Bin. Tokyo: Chikuma shobô, 1970.

70.   . Brunos Drøm. Trans. by Inger-Sophie Manthey. Oslo: Gyldendal, 1970.

71.   . Bruno's Drøm. Trans. by Vibeke Willumsen. Copenhagen: Nyt Nordisk Forlag, n. d.

72.   . Bruno's Droom. Trans. by Clara Eggink. Amsterdam: Contact, 1970.

73.   . Le Rêve de Bruno. Trans. by Jean Quéval. Paris: Gallimard, 1972.

74.   . Il Songo di Bruno. Trans. by Gabriella Fiori Andreini. Milan: Feltrinelli, 1971.

Reviews of Bruno's Dream

75. Anonymous. British Book News [no number] (April 1969):325.

76.   . New Yorker 44 (1 February 1969):90.

77.   . Publishers Weekly 194 (4 November 1968):48.

78.   . Virginia Quarterly Review 45 (Summer 1969):xcii.

79. Allen, Walter. New York Times Book Review, 19 January 1969, pp. 5, 34.

80. Blackburn, Sara. Nation 208 (27 January 1969): 124.

81. Garis, Robert. Hudson Review 22 (Spring 1969): 148, 161-63.

82. Griffin, L. W. Library Journal 93 (15 December 1968):4664.

83. Halio, J. L. Southern Review [Baton Rouge, Louisiana] 7 (Spring 1971):635.

84. Hill, W. B. America 120 (3 May 1969):538.

85. _____. Best Sellers 28 (15 January 1969):426.

86. Jackson, Katherine Gauss. Harper's Magazine 238 (February 1969):102-103.

87. Kuehl, Linda. Commonweal 90 (28 March 1969): 52-53.

88. McDowell, Frederick P. W. Contemporary Literature 11 (Summer 1970):421-24.

89. Price, Martin. Yale Review 58 (March 1969): 466.

90. Weeks, Edward. Atlantic Monthly 223 (February 1969):129.

91. Williams, David. Punch 256 (15 January 1969): 106.

92. A Fairly Honourable Defeat. Greenwich, Conn.: Fawcett Publications, Inc., 1973.
Harmondsworth, Middlesex, England: Penguin Books, Ltd., 1972, paperback.
London: Chatto & Windus, Ltd., 1st ed., 1970.
New York: Viking Press, 1970 and Fawcett World Library, 1973, 1974, paperback.
Toronto: Clarke, Irwin & Company, Ltd., 1970.

Translations of A Fairly Honourable Defeat

93. Murdoch, Iris. Une Défaite Assez Honorable. Trans. by Yvonne Davet. Paris: Gallimard, 1972.

94. _____. Een Nogal Eervolle Aftocht. Trans. by Clara Eggink. Amsterdam: Uitgeverij Contact, 1971.

Reviews of A Fairly Honourable Defeat

95. Anonymous. Best Sellers 32 (1 February 1973): 503.

96. _____. British Book News [no number] (April 1970):338.

97. _____. Choice 7 (June 1970):545.

98. Avant, John A. Library Journal 94 (15 December 1969):4539.

99. Culligan, Glendy. Saturday Review 53 (7 February 1970):37-38.

100. Gray, P. E. Yale Review 60 (October 1970): 102.

101. Lipscomb, Elizabeth Johnston. In Masterplots 1972 Annual, pp. 134-37. Ed. by Frank N. Magill. Englewood Cliffs, N.J.: Salem Press, 1972.

102. The Flight from the Enchanter. Harmondsworth, Middlesex, England: Penguin Books, Ltd., 1962, 1969, paperback.
London: Chatto & Windus, Ltd., 1st ed., 1955, 1956. New York: Viking Press, 1956, 1965; Viking Press, Compass Books, 1956, 1969, paperback; and Warner Paperback Library, 1973, 1974, paperback.

Translations of The Flight from the Enchanter

103. Murdoch, Iris. Flucht vor dem Zauberer. Trans. by Werner Peterich. Munich: R. Piper, 1964.

104. _____. Huyendo del Encantador. Trans. by Jorge Ferrer Aleu. Barcelona and Buenos Aires: Plaza & Janés, 1964.

105. _____. Majutsushi Kara Nogarete. Trans. by Inouchi Yūshiro. Tokyo: Taiyosha, n.d. [ca. 1968].

106. _____. Le Séducteur Quitté. Trans. by A. Arax Der Nersessian. Paris: Editions Gallimard, 1964.

Reviews of The Flight from the Enchanter

107. Anonymous. Booklist 52 (1 May 1965):363.

108. _____. British Book News no. 190 (June 1956):386.

109.   . Cambridge Review [England] 78 (9
      June 1956):685, 687.

110.   . Kirkus Reviews 24 (15 February
      1956):141.

111.   . Masterplots 1957 Annual. Ed. by
      Frank N. Magill. New York: Salem Press,
      1957, pp. 70-72. Also in Survey of Contem-
      porary Literature, vol. 3, pp. 1584-86. Ed.
      by Frank N. Magill. New York: Salem Press,
      1971.

112.   . New Yorker 32 (12 May 1956):161.

113.   . Saturday Review 48 (26 June 1965):
      42.

114. Aaron, Daniel. Hudson Review 9 (Winter 1956-
      57):624-25.

115. Bostock, Anna. Manchester Guardian, 27
      March 1956, p. 4.

116. Doherty, Paul C. America 130 (9 February
      1974):93.

117. Engle, Paul. Chicago Tribune Books Today,
      17 June 1956, p. 3.

118. George, Daniel. Spectator 196 (30 March
      1956):418.

119. Hughes, Riley. Catholic World 183 (July
      1956):313.

120. Rhodes, Anthony. Listener 55 (19 April 1956):
      475.

121. Richardson, Maurice. New Statesman and Na-
      tion 51 (31 March 1956):315.

122. Van Ghent, Dorothy. Yale Review 46 (Autumn
      1956):153-55.

123. Webster, Harvey Curtis. Saturday Review 39
      (21 April 1956):14.

Tamara Meldsted. Copenhagen: Nyt Nordisk Forlag-A. Busck, 1966.

175. _____. Rood en Groen. Trans. by N. Funke-Bordewijk. Amsterdam/Antwerpen: Uitgeverij Contact, 1966.

176. _____. Il Rosso e il Verde. Trans. by Gabriella Fiori Andreini. Milan: Feltrinelli, 1967.

177. _____. Rött och Grönt. Trans. by Magda Lagerman. Stockholm: P. A. Norstedt & Sonners Forlag, 1969.

Reviews of The Red and the Green

178. Anonymous. Booklist 62 (1 December 1965): 355.

179. _____. British Book News no. 305 (January 1966):79-80.

180. _____. Choice 3 (June 1966):310.

181. _____. Kirkus Reviews 33 (1 August 1965): 789.

182. _____. New Yorker 41 (8 January 1966):111.

183. _____. Virginia Quarterly Review 42 (Spring 1966):xlviii, lii.

184. Clarke, J. J. Best Sellers 25 (15 November 1965):324.

185. Cook, B. Extension 60 (January 1966):46.

186. Cook, Roderick. Harper's Magazine 231 (November 1965):129.

187. Fleischer, Leonore. Publishers Weekly 190 (26 September 1966):136.

188. Fytton, Francis. London Magazine n. s. 5 (November 1965):99-100.

189. Griffin, L. W. Library Journal 90 (1

November 1965):4807.

190.   Leone, A. T.   Catholic World 203 (June 1966):
        188.

191.   Ostermann, Robert.   National Observer, 8
        November 1965. p. 22.

192.   Pell, E.   New Leader 48 (20 December 1965):
        19.

193.   Price, R. G. G.   Punch 249 (27 October 1965):
        625.

194.   Sale, Roger.   Hudson Review 19 (Spring 1966):
        124, 128-29.

195.   Sheed, Wilfrid.   Life 59 (5 November 1965):15.

196.   Sidnell, M. J.   Canadian Forum 46 (October
        1966):166.

197.   Trachtenberg, S.   Yale Review 55 (Spring
        1966):444.

198.   Wardle, I.   Observer [London], 17 October
        1965, p. 28.

199.   Webb, W. L.   Manchester Guardian Weekly,
        21 October 1965, p. 11.

200.   Whittington-Egan, R.   Books and Bookmen 11
        (December 1965):40.

201. The Sacred and Profane Love Machine.   London:
      Chatto & Windus, Ltd., 1st ed., April 1974.
      New York: Viking Press, September 1974.

Reviews of The Sacred and Profane Love Machine

202.   Anonymous.   Booklist 71 (1 December 1974):
        367.

203.   _____ .   Books and Bookmen 19 (June 1974):
        85.

204.   _____ .   Choice 11 (July 1974):762.

205. _____ . Choice 12 (March 1975):76-77.

206. _____ . Economist 251 (13 April 1974):73.

207. _____ . Kirkus Reviews 42 (15 July 1974):
761.

208. _____ . New York Times Book Review, 1
December 1974, p. 70.

209. _____ . Publishers Weekly 206 (5 August
1974):51.

210. _____ . Washington Post Book World, 8
December 1974, p. 1.

211. Avant, John A. Library Journal 99 (August
1974):1985.

212. Betsky, Celia. New Republic 171 (14 September 1974):28-29.

213. Hill, W. B. America 131 (16 November 1974):
301.

214. O'Hara, T. Best Sellers 34 (1 October 1974):
297.

215. The Sandcastle. Harmondsworth, Middlesex, England:
Penguin Books, Ltd., 1960, 1968, 1971, paperback.
London: Chatto & Windus, Ltd., 1st ed., 1957 and
Chatto & Windus (Educational) Ltd., Books for Today
Series, 1969, paperback.
New York: Viking Press, 1957 and Warner Paperback
Library, 1973, 1974, paperback.
Toronto: Clarke, Irwin & Company, Ltd., 1957.

Translations of The Sandcastle

216. Murdoch, Iris. El Castillo de Arena. Trans.
by Jorge Ferrer Aleu. Barcelona: Plaza &
Janés, 1964.

217. _____ . Grad Iz Peska. Trans. by Majda
Stanovink. Ljubljana, Yugoslavia: Državna
založba Slovenije, 1964.

218. _____ . Hiekkalinna. Trans. by Mikko

Kilpi.   Porvoo, Finland: W. Söderström,
1957, 1965.

219. _____. Hrad z Písku.   Trans. by Helena
Prokopová.   Praha, Czechoslovakia: Mladá
Fronta, 1972.

220. _____. Sandslottet.   Trans. by Olov.
Jonason.   Stockholm: Norstedt (Ny utg.), n. d.
[ca. 1964].

221. _____. Sandslottet.   Trans. by Inger-
Sophie Manthey.   Oslo: Bokklubben, n. d.
[ca. 1964].

222. _____. Sandslottet.   Trans. by Michael
Tejn.   Copenhagen: Schønbergske, 1968.

223. _____. Die Sandburg.   Trans. by Maria
Wolff.   Berlin; Darmstadt: Dt. Buch-Gemein-
schaft, n. d.

224. _____. Suna No Shiro.   Trans. by Kurihara
Yukio.   Tokyo: Taiyôsha, n. d. [ca. 1967].

225. _____. Op Zand Gebound.   Trans. by E.
Veegens-Latorf.   Amsterdam: Contact, 1963,
1969.

Reviews of The Sandcastle

226. Anonymous.   Booklist 53 (1 April 1957):394.

227. _____. Booklist 53 (15 May 1957):478.

228. _____. Bookmark 16 (June 1957):214.

229. _____. British Book News no. 203 (July
1957):451.

230. _____. British Book News no. 243 (November 1960):832.

231. Bryden, Ronald.   Listener 57 (16 May 1956):
800.

232. Engle, Paul.   Chicago Tribune Books Today,
30 June 1957, p. 4.

233.   George, Daniel. <u>Spectator</u> 198 (17 May 1957):
       657.

234.   Harvey, W. J. <u>Essays in Criticism</u> 8 (April
       1958):186.

235.   Hoey, R. A. <u>Library Journal</u> 82 (15 April
       1957):1067.

236.   McLaughlin, Richard. <u>Springfield Republican,</u>
       14 July 1957, p. 5C.

237.   Paulding, Gouverneur. <u>New York Herald
       Tribune Book Review,</u> 12 May 1957, p. 5.

238.   Price, Martin. <u>Yale Review</u> 47 (Autumn 1957):
       146-48.

239.   Richardson, Maurice. <u>New Statesman and Na-
       tion</u> 53 (11 May 1957):616.

240.   Shrapnel, Norman. <u>Manchester Guardian,</u> 28
       May 1957, p. 4.

241. A Severed Head. Harmondsworth, Middlesex, Eng-
      land: Penguin Books, Ltd., 1961, 1967, 1969, paper-
      back.
      London: Chatto & Windus, Ltd., 1961. 1st ed.,
      1961.
      New York: Avon Books, Bard edition, 1961, 1966,
      1970, 1974, paperback; Viking Press, 1961; and Viking
      Press, Compass Books, 1963, 1974, paperback.

            Translations of <u>A Severed Head</u>

242.   Murdoch, Iris. <u>Een Afgehouwen Hoofd.</u> Trans.
       by H. W. J. Schaap. Amsterdam: Uitgeverij
       Contact, 1965, 1968.

243.   _____. <u>Et Afhugget Hoved.</u> Trans. by
       Michael Tejn. Copenhagen: Nyt Nordisk
       Forlag-A. Busck, 1963.

244.   _____. <u>Et Avhugget Hode.</u> Trans. by
       Inger-Sophie Manthey. Oslo: Gyldendal Norsk
       Forlag, 1962.

245.   _____. <u>Cabeza Cercenada.</u> Trans. by

Jorge Ferrer-Vidal. Buenos Aires: Plaza &
Janés, S. A., 1964.

246.　　　　　　. Maskenspiel. Trans. by Karin
Reese. Munich: R. Piper, 1963.

247.　　　　　　. Meng Ching. Trans. by Ho Hsin.
Taipei: Student's Book Co., 2 vols, n. d. [ca.
1967].

248.　　　　　　. Una Testa Tagliata. Trans. by
Valerio Riva. Milan: Feltrinelli, 1963.

249.　　　　　　. Une Tête Coupée. Trans. by
Yvonne Davet. Paris: Gallimard, 1966.

Reviews of A Severed Head

250. Anonymous. Booklist 57 (1 May 1961):546.

251.　　　　　　. Books of the Month [London], July
1961, p. 15.

252.　　　　　　. British Book News no. 253 (September 1961):674-75.

253.　　　　　　. British Book News no. 285 (May
1964):365.

254.　　　　　　. Kirkus Reviews 29 (1 February
1961):129.

255.　　　　　　. Masterplots 1962 Annual, pp. 266-
68. Ed. by Frank N. Magill. New York:
Salem Press, 1962. Also in Survey of Con-
temporary Literature, vol. 6, pp. 4233-35.
Ed. by Frank N. Magill. New York: Salem
Press, 1971.

256.　　　　　　. Times [London], 15 June 1961, p.
17.

257. Everett, Barbara. Critical Quarterly [Man-
chester, England] 3 (Autumn 1961):270-71.

258. Falle, George. Canadian Forum 41 (November 1961):187.

259. Georgi, Charlotte. <u>Library Journal</u> 86 (1 April 1961):1479.

260. Hobson, Harold. <u>Christian Science Monitor</u>, 22 June 1961, p. 7.

261. McLaughlin, Richard. <u>Springfield Republican</u> [Springfield, Mass.], 4 June 1961, p. 4D.

262. Singer, Burns. <u>Listener</u> 65 (15 June 1961): 1061.

263. Warnke, F. J. <u>Yale Review</u> 50 (June 1961): 632-33.

264. <u>The Time of the Angels.</u> Harmondsworth, Middlesex, England: Penguin Books, Ltd., 1966, 1968, 1971, paperback.
London: Chatto & Windus, Ltd., 1st ed., 1966.
New York: Viking Press, 1966 and Avon Books, Bard edition, 1971, 1974, paperback.
Toronto: Clarke, Irwin & Company, Ltd., 1966.

Translations of <u>The Time of the Angels</u>

265. Murdoch, Iris. <u>Les Angéliques.</u> Trans. by Anne-Marie Soulac. Paris: Mercure de France, 1969.

266. _____. <u>Änglarnas Tid.</u> Trans. by Maj Lorents. Stockholm: P. A. Norstedt & Soners Förlag, 1967.

267. _____. <u>Czas Aniołów.</u> Trans. by Agnieszka Glinczanka. Warsaw: Państw. Instytut Wydawn, 1970.

268. _____. <u>Englenes Tid.</u> Trans. by Inger-Sophie Manthey. Oslo: Gyldendal Norsk Förlag, 1967.

269. _____. <u>Enkelten Aika.</u> Trans. by Eila Pennanen. Porvoo, Helsinki: W. Söderström Osakeyhtiö, 1969.

270. _____. <u>Praest Unden Gud.</u> Trans. by Karina Windfeld-Hansen. Copenhagen: Nyt Nordisk Forlag-A. Busck, 1967.

271.   . Il Tempo degli Angeli.   Trans. by
Gabriella Fiori Andreini.   Milan: Feltrinelli,
1972.

272.   . Tenshi Tachi No Toki.   Trans. by
Ishida Kôtarô.   Tokyo: Chikuma shobô, n. d.
[ca. 1967].

273.   . De Tijd van de Engelen.   Trans.
by Clara Eggink.   Amsterdam: Contact, n. d.
[ca. 1967].

Reviews of The Time of the Angels

274.   Anonymous.   Best Sellers 31 (1 February
1972):495.

275.   . Booklist 63 (1 September 1966):34.

276.   . Books Abroad 41 (Spring 1967):221.

277.   . British Book News no. 315 (November 1966):869-70.

278.   . Choice 4 (May 1967):290.

279.   . Kirkus Reviews 34 (15 July 1966):
706.

280.   . National Observer, 12 September
1966, p. 23.

281.   . Newsweek 68 (26 September 1966):
118.

282.   Cook, Roderick.   Harper's Magazine 233
(November 1966):141-42.

283.   Cruttwell, Patrick.   Hudson Review 20 (Spring
1967):163, 174, 176.

284.   Fleischer, Leonore.   Publishers Weekly 192
(23 October 1967):53.

285.   Griffin, L. W.   Library Journal 91 (1 September 1966):3973.

286. Hill, W. B. America 115 (26 November 1966): 707.

287. Kitching, J. Publishers Weekly 190 (25 July 1966):70.

288. Lipnack, Linda Victoria. Commonweal 85 (13 January 1967):408.

289. Moore, H. T. Chicago Tribune Books Today, 9 October 1966, p. 5.

290. Muggeridge, M. Esquire 67 (February 1967): 50.

291. Phillipson, J. S. Best Sellers 26 (1 October 1966):236.

292. Rosenthal, R. New Leader 49 (24 October 1966):21.

293. Under the Net. Harmondsworth, Middlesex, England: Penguin Books, Ltd., 1960, 1971, paperback.
London: Chatto & Windus, Ltd., 1st ed., 1954, 1956 and Longman Group, Ltd., Heritage of Literature Series, 1966, paperback.
New York: Viking Press, 1954; Avon Books, 1967, 1974, paperback; and Viking Press, Compass Books, 1964, 1974, paperback.
Toronto: Clarke, Irwin & Company, Ltd., 1954.

Translations of Under the Net

294. Murdoch, Iris. Ami No Naka. Trans. by Suzuki Yasushi. Tokyo: Hakusuisha, n.d. [ca. 1965].

295. _____. Bajo la Red. Trans. by M. Consuelo Gironés. Barcelona: Diamante, 1962. Buenos Aires: Plaza & Janés, n.d.

296. _____. Dans le Filet. Trans. by Clara Malraux. Paris: Librairie Plon, 1954, 1957.

297. _____. I Gatti Ci Guardano. Trans. by Gaby Goering. Milan: Garzanti, 1956.

298. _____. A Háló Alatt. Trans. by Bati Laszlo. Budapest: Magveto Kiado, 1971.

299. _____. Onder het Net. Trans. by Clara Eggink. Amsterdam: Uitgeverij Contact, 1972.

300. _____. Pod Mrežata. Trans. by Katja Gončarova. Sofia, Bulgaria: Nar. Mladež, 1970.

301. _____. Pod Set°ju. Trans. by M. Lorie. Moscow: Progress, n. d. [ca. 1966].

302. _____. Pod Síti. Trans. by Eliška Hornátová. Praha, Czechoslovakia: Odeon, n. d.

303. _____. Sotto la Rete. Trans. by Argia Micchettoni. Milan: Garzanti, 1966.

304. _____. Soto la Xarza. Trans. by Montserrat Abelló. Barcelona: Edicions Proa., 1965.

305. _____. Unter dem Netz. Trans. by Ilse Krämer. Frankfurt am Main: Fischer Bücherei, 1957, 1962. Published as Vol. 463 of Fischer Bücherei.

Reviews of Under the Net

306. Anonymous. Booklist 50 (15 May 1954):359.

307. _____. British Book News no. 168 (August 1954):466.

308. _____. New Yorker 30 (12 June 1954):106-107.

309. Amis, Kingsley. Spectator 192 (11 June 1954):722.

310. Fitzsimmons, T. Sewanee Review 63 (Spring 1955):328-30.

311. Fleischer, Leonore. Publishers Weekly 191

(30 January 1967):113.

312. Fox, Joan. Canadian Forum 34 (October 1954): 164.

313. Grigorov, Georgi M. Plamăk [Sofia] 14 (1970): 93.

314. Holzhauer, Jean. Kirkus Reviews 22 (15 March 1954):207.

315. Keelan, B. C. L. Books of the Month [London], August 1954, p. 19.

316. McLaughlin, Richard. Springfield Republican, 13 June 1954, p. 7C.

317. Petersen, Clarence. Chicago Tribune Books Today, 26 March 1967, p. 9.

318. Raymond, John. New Statesman and Nation 47 (5 June 1954):737-38.

319. Walbridge, E. F. Library Journal 79 (15 April 1954):771.

320. Wilson, Angus. Observer [London], 6 June 1954, p. 7.

321. The Unicorn. Harmondsworth, Middlesex, England: Penguin Books, Ltd., 1966, 1971, paperback.
London: Chatto & Windus, Ltd., 1st ed., 1963.
New York: Avon Books, Bard edition, 1974, paperback.
Toronto: Clarke, Irwin & Company, Ltd., 1963.

Translations of The Unicorn

322. Murdoch, Iris. De Eenhoorn. Trans. by N. Funke-Bordewijk. Amsterdam and Antwerpen: Uitgeverij Contact, 1965; and Amsterdam: Contact, 1968.

323. _____. Enhjørningen. Trans. by Karen Meldsted. Copenhagen: Nyt Nordisk Forlag-A. Busck, 1964.

324. _____. Enhörningen. Trans. by Maj

Lorents. Stockholm: P. A. Norstedt &
Söners Förlag, 1967.

325.   . Le Château de la Licorne. Trans.
by Anne-Marie Soulac. Paris: Mercure de
France, 1965.

326.   . La Sue Parte di Colpa. [No trans.
given.] Milan: Feltrinelli, 2nd ed., 1969.

327.   . El Unicornio. Trans. by Vida
Ozores. Mexico: J. Mortiz, 1966.

328.   . Yksisarvinen. Trans. by Eila
Pennanen. Porvoo, Helsinki: W. Söderström
Osakeyhtiö, 1964.

Reviews of The Unicorn

329. Anonymous. Booklist 59 (15 April 1963):679.

330.   . British Book News no. 280 (December 1963):920.

331. Davenport, G. National Review 14 (18 June
1963):505.

332. Frye, D. Ramparts 2 (Winter 1964):91.

333. Hill, W. B. America 109 (23 November 1963):
682.

334. Hobson, Harold. Christian Science Monitor,
9 May 1963, p. 8B.

335. Jackson, R. B. Library Journal 88 (15 April
1963):1688.

336. Murray, J. G. Critic 21 (June 1963):77.

337. Siggins, C. M. Best Sellers 23 (15 May
1963):71.

338. Webster, Harvey Curtis. In Masterplots 1964
Annual, pp. 281-83. Ed. by Frank N. Magill.
New York: Salem Press, 1964. Also in
Survey of Contemporary Literature, vol. 7,

pp. 4828-30. Ed. by Frank N. Magill. New York: Salem Press, 1971.

339. An Unofficial Rose. Harmondsworth, Middlesex, England: Penguin Books, Ltd., 1962, 1964, 1966, 1971, paperback. London: Chatto & Windus, Ltd., 1st ed., 1962 and Reprint Society, 1962, 1964. New York: Viking Press, 1962 and Warner Paperback Library, 1973, 1974, paperback. Toronto: Clarke, Irwin & Company, Ltd., 1962.

Translations of An Unofficial Rose

340. Murdoch, Iris. Epävirallinen Ruusu. Trans. by Eila Pennanen. Porvoo, Helsinki: W. Söderström Osakeyhtiö, 1963.

341. _____. Une Rose Anonyme. Trans. by Anne-Marie Soulac. Vienna: Gallimard, 1966.

342. _____. En Uoffisiell Rose. Trans. by Michael Tejn. Copenhagen: Nyt Nordisk Forlag-A. Busck, 1964.

343. _____. En Uofficiel Rose. Trans. by Inger-Sophie Manthey. Oslo: Gyldendal Norsk Forlag, 1963.

344. _____. Warde Ahava. Trans. by M. Weiseltier. Tel-Aviv: Amichai, 1963.

345. _____. Een Wilde Roos. Trans. by Katja Vranken. Amsterdam: Uitgeverij Contact N. V., 1964, 1970.

Reviews of An Unofficial Rose

346. Anonymous. Booklist 58 (15 May 1962):645.

347. _____. Bookmark [New York State Library, Albany] 21 (May 1962):223.

348. _____. British Book News no. 266 (October 1962):750.

349. _____. Kirkus Reviews 30 (1 March 1962): 258.

350. _____. Masterplots 1963 Annual, pp. 276-79. Ed. by Frank N. Magill. New York: Salem Press, 1963. Also in Survey of Contemporary Literature, vol. 7, pp. 4841-44. Ed. by Frank N. Magill. New York: Salem Press, 1971.

351. Balliet, Whitney. New Yorker 38 (15 September 1962):178.

352. Bradbury, Malcolm. Punch 242 (27 June 1962): 989-90.

353. Engle, Paul. Chicago Tribune Books Today, 17 June 1962, p. 3.

354. Hagler, Margaret. Books Abroad 37 (Winter 1963):80.

355. Jackson, R. B. Library Journal 87 (15 April 1962):1630.

356. Paulding, Gouverneur. New York Herald Tribune Books, 17 June 1962, pp. 4-5.

357. A Word Child. London: Chatto & Windus, Ltd., 1975.

B. CRITICAL ESSAYS

358. "Against Dryness: A Polemical Sketch. " Encounter 16 (January 1961):16-20.

359. "Arts and Morals. " Unpublished lecture delivered at Zurich University, 12 March 1968. Also in Barbara Stettler-Imfeld, The Adolescent in the Novels of Iris Murdoch, p. 152. Zürich: Juris Druck, 1970.

360. "The Existentialist Hero. " Listener 43 (23 March 1950):523-24.

361. "The Existentialist Political Myth. " Socratic 5 (1952): 52.

362. "Full Circle. " New Statesman and Nation 21 (3 May 1941):460-61.

363. "A House of Theory. " In Conviction, pp. 218-33. Ed. by Norman Mackenzie. London: MacGibbon & Kee, 1958; reprinted in Partisan Review 26 (Winter 1959):17-31.

364. "The Idea of Perfection. " Yale Review 53 (March 1964):342-80.

365. "Important Things. " In Encore: The Sunday Times Book, pp. 299-301. Ed. by Leonard Russell. London: Michael Joseph, 1963.

366. "Metaphysics and Ethics. " In The Nature of Metaphysics, pp. 99-123. Ed. by D. F. Pears. London: Macmillan & Company, Ltd. , 1957, and New York: St. Martin's Press, Inc. , 1965.

367. "The Moral Decision About Homosexuality. " Man and Society [London] 7 (Summer 1964):3-6.

368. "Nostalgia for the Particular. " Proceedings of the

Aristotelian Society 52 (9 June 1952):243-60.

369.   "The Novelist as Metaphysician. " Listener 43 (16
       March 1950):473, 476.

370.   "Of 'God' and 'Good.' " In The Anatomy of Knowledge,
       pp. 233-58. Ed. by Marjorie Grene. Amherst,
       Mass.: University of Massachusetts Press, 1969.
       [Paper delivered by Iris Murdoch at the Meeting of
       the Study Group on Foundations of Cultural Unity,
       Bowdoin College, Maine, August 1966.]

371.   "Political Morality. " Listener 78 (21 September
       1967):353-54.

372.   "Salvation by Words. " New York Review of Books
       18 (15 June 1972):3-8.

373.   Sartre: Romantic Rationalist. Cambridge, England:
       Bowes & Bowes Publishers, Ltd., 1st ed., 1953,
       1961, 1965, paperback.
       London: William Collins, Sons & Co., Ltd., 1953,
       1969, paperback and Fontana Books, 1967, paperback.
       New Haven: Yale University Press, 1953, 1959, 1967,
       1974, paperback.
       Toronto: British Book Service, Ltd., 1953 and Burns
       & MacEachern, Ltd., 1953, 1959, paperback.

       Translations of Sartre: Romantic Rationalist

       374.   Murdoch, Iris. Sartre, Romantic Gôri
              Shugisha. Trans. by Tanaka Seitarô and
              Nakaota Hiroshi. Tokyo: Kokubunsha, n. d.
              [ca. 1967].

       375.   _____ . Sartre, Un Racionalista Romántico.
              Trans. by Roberto Eugenio Bixio. Buenos
              Aires: Editorial Sur, 1956.

       376.   _____ . Sartre, Yazarligi Ve Felsefesi.
              Trans. by Selâhattin Hilâv. Istanbul: De
              Yayinevi, 1964.

       Reviews of Sartre: Romantic Rationalist

       377.   Anonymous. British Book News no. 161
              (January 1954):48.

378.   Clark, A. F. B.   Canadian Forum 34 (April
        1954):19-20.

379.   Roland, Albert.   Books Abroad 28 (Autumn
        1954):481.

380.   Williams, R.   Manchester Guardian Weekly,
        18 May 1967, p. 11.

381.   The Sovereignty of Good.   London: Routledge & Kegan
        Paul, Ltd. , Studies in Ethics and Philosophy of Reli-
        gion Series, 1st ed. , 1970, hardbound and paperback.
        New York: Schocken Books, Studies in Ethics and the
        Philosophy of Religion Series, 1970, 1971, 1974, hard-
        bound and paperback.

                Reviews of The Sovereignty of Good

382.   Anonymous.   British Book News [no number]
        (February 1971):99.

383.   .   Christian Century 88 (31 March
        1971):410.

384.   Coventry, John.   Heythrop Journal 12 (April
        1971):202-203.

385.   Cummings, P. W.   Library Journal 96 (15
        April 1971):1372.

386.   Downey, Berchmans.   Best Sellers 31 (1 April
        1971):8.

387.   Gunton, Colin.   Religious Studies 8 (June 1972):
        180-81.

388.   Kleinig, J.   Australasian Journal of Philosophy
        [Sydney] 49 (May 1971):112.

389.   Mounce, H. O.   Philosophy 47 (April 1972):
        178-80.

390.   Tylee, Claire.   Philosophical Books [Leicester,
        England] 12 (October 1971):18.

391.   The Sovereignty of Good over Other Concepts.   [The
        Leslie Stephen Lecture, 1967] Cambridge, England:

Cambridge University Press, 1967.

Reviews of The Sovereignty of Good
          over Other Concepts

392.   Anonymous.   Ethics 79 (January 1969):171.

393.   Kenny, Anthony.   Notes and Queries n. s. 18
       (October 1971):389-90.

394.   "Speaking of Writing. "   Times [London], 13 February
       1964, p. 15.

395.   "The Sublime and the Beautiful Revisited. "   Yale Re-
       view 49 (December 1959):247-51.

396.   "The Sublime and the Good. "   Chicago Review 13
       (Autumn 1959):42-55.

397.   "T. S. Eliot as a Moralist. "   In T. S. Eliot: A
       Symposium for his Seventieth Birthday, pp. 152-60.
       Ed. by Neville Braybrooke.   London: Rupert Hart-
       Davis, 1958.

398.   "Vision and Choice in Morality. "   Proceedings of the
       Aristotelian Society: Dreams and Self-Knowledge Sup-
       plement 30 (London 1956):32-58.

399.   Murdoch, Iris; Hampshire, S. N. ; Gardiner, P. L. ;
       and Pears, D. F.   "Freedom and Knowledge. "   In
       Freedom and the Will, pp. 80-104.   Ed. by D. F.
       Pears.   New York: St. Martin's Press, Inc. , 1963.
       [Most of the essays in this book originated as talks
       in the Third Programme of the B. B. C. , in which Iris
       Murdoch participated.]

400.   Murdoch, Iris; Lloyd, A. C. ; and Ryle, Gilbert.
       "Symposium: Thinking and Language. "   Proceedings
       of the Aristotelian Society Supplement 25 (1951):25-82.
       [Murdoch's contribution to the Symposium, pp. 25-34.]

C. PLAYS

401. Murdoch, Iris, and Saunders, James. "The Italian Girl. " First performance at the Bristol Old Vic Theatre, Bristol, in December 1967. Opened at Wyndham's Theatre, London, on 1 February 1968.

402. _____. The Italian Girl [acting edition]. London: Samuel French, Ltd. , 1968.

403. _____. The Italian Girl. [Complete text of the acting version of the play.] Play and Players 15 (March 1968):27-42, 53-60, 62, 65.

Reviews of "The Italian Girl"

404. Anonymous. The Italian Girl. In Play Index: 1968-1972, p. 267. Ed. by Estelle A. Fidell. New York: The H. W. Wilson Company, 1973. [Brief description of the acting version.]

405. Barnes, Clive. New York Times Theater Reviews, v. 8/1967-1970, 4 July 1968. [Performed at Wyndham's Theatre, London, 3 July 1968.]

406. Murdoch, Iris. "The Servants and the Snow. " Produced in Greenwich, 1970 and London, 1970.

407. _____. The Servants and the Snow. London: Chatto & Windus, Ltd. , 1st ed. , 1973. New York: Viking Press, March 1974.

Review of "The Servants and the Snow"

408. Harding, W. J. Library Journal 99 (15 April 1974):1148.

409. Murdoch, Iris, and Priestley, John B. "A Severed

35

Head." First performance in Great Britain given at
The Theatre Royal, Bristol, 7 May 1963, by The
Bristol Old Vic Company. Produced in London, 1963
and New York, 1964.

410.   . A Severed Head. London: Chatto &
Windus, Ltd., 1964.
Toronto: Clarke, Irwin & Company, Ltd., 1964.
London: Samuel French, Ltd., 1964.

411.   . A Severed Head. In Plays of the Sixties,
vol. 2, pp. 13-101. Ed. by J. M. Charlton. London:
Pan Books Ltd., 1967. [Reading edition of the script
used at The Criterion Theatre, London, 1963.]

Reviews of "A Severed Head"

412.   Dent, Allan. "At the Play." Punch 244 (22
        May 1963):751. [Review of Theatre Royal pro-
        duction in Bristol.]

413.   Downes-Panter, Mollie. New Yorker 39 (7
        September 1963):96, 98.

414.   Kerr, Walter. New York Theatre Critics' Re-
        views 25 (9 November 1964):178-79. [Review
        of The Royal Theater production in New York.]

415.   Taubman, Howard. New York Times Theater
        Reviews. V.7/1960-1966, 29 October 1964.
        [Pages are not numbered.] [Review of The
        Royal Theater production in New York.]

416.   Worsley, T. C. New York Times Theater
        Reviews. V.7/1960-1966, June 1963. [Pages
        are not numbered.] [Review of performance
        at The Criterion Theatre, London, 27 June
        1963.]

417. Murdoch, Iris. "The Three Arrows." Produced at
      Arts Theatre, Cambridge, England, 1972.

418.   . The Three Arrows. Bound with The Ser-
      vants and the Snow. London: Chatto & Windus, Ltd.,
      1973. New York: Viking Press, 1974.

Reviews of "The Three Arrows"

419.   Anonymous.   British Book News [no number]
       (January 1974):58.

420.   _____. Publishers Weekly 205 (25 February
       1974):106.

D. SHORT STORIES

421.   Murdoch, Iris. "Something Special. " In Winter's
        Tales 3, pp. 175-204. [No editor given.] London:
        Macmillan & Company, Ltd. and New York: St.
        Martin's Press, Inc., 1957.

422.   _____ . "The Time of the Angels. " Cosmopolitan
        162 (January 1967):103-105. [Chapter IV of the novel
        The Time of the Angels by Iris Murdoch.]

E. BOOK REVIEWS

423.   Murdoch, Iris. "At One Remove from Tragedy." Nation 182 (9 June 1956):493-94. [Review of The Mandarins by Simone de Beauvoir, trans. from the French by Leonard M. Friedman.]

424.   _____. "The Darkness of Practical Reason." Encounter 27 (July 1966):46-50. [Review of Freedom of the Individual by Stuart Hampshire.]

425.   _____. "Hegel in Modern Dress." Spectator 53 (25 May 1957):675-76. [Review of Being and Nothingness by Jean-Paul Sartre, trans. from the French by Hazel E. Barnes.]

426.   _____. "Knowing the Void." Spectator 197 (2 November 1956):613-14. [Review of The Notebooks of Simone Weil, trans. from the French and ed. by Arthur Wills.]

427.   _____. "Mass, Might and Myth." Spectator 209 (7 September 1962):337-38. [Review of Crowds and Power by Elias Canetti and trans. from the German by Carol Stewart.]

428.   _____. "Mr. Gellner's Game." Observer [London], Christmas Books, 29 November 1959, p. 5. [Review of Words and Things by Ernest Gellner.]

PART II

WRITINGS ABOUT
IRIS MURDOCH

A. BOOKS

429. Allen, Walter Ernest. The Modern Novel in Britain and the United States. New York: E. P. Dutton & Co., Inc., 1964, 1965, pp. 278, 282-84. [On Iris Murdoch's earlier novels.]

430. _____. Reading a Novel. London: Phoenix House, 1949 and rev. ed., 1956, pp. 61-64. [The Bell]

431. _____. Tradition and Dream: The English and American Novel from the Twenties to our Time. London: Phoenix House, 1964, pp. 278, 282-84. [The Bell, The Flight from the Enchanter, A Severed Head, Under the Net]

432. Allsop, Kenneth. The Angry Decade: A Survey of the Cultural Revolt of the Nineteen-Fifties. Birkenhead, England: Willmer Bros. & Haram, Ltd., 1958; London: P. Owen, 1958; and New York: The British Book Centre, 1958, pp. 88-95. [The Flight from the Enchanter, Under the Net]

433. Baldanza, Frank. Iris Murdoch. New York: Twayne Publishers, Inc., 1974, 187p. Reviewed by Emily T. Berges in Library Journal 99 (1 May 1974):1301, by Bernard F. Dick in Books Abroad 44 (Spring 1975): 328, and anonymously in Choice 12 (March 1975):68. [Murdoch's fifteen novels discussed in chronological order, along with these major critical essays: "Against Dryness: A Polemical Sketch," "A House of Theory," "The Idea of Perfection," "The Sovereignty of Good over Other Concepts," "The Sublime and the Beautiful Revisited," "The Sublime and the Good," and "Vision and Choice in Morality."]

434. Bergonzi, Bernard. The Situation of the Novel. London: Macmillan & Company, Ltd., and Pittsburgh: University of Pittsburgh Press, 1970, pp. 47-49, 50, 52, 60, 75, 194. ["Against Dryness," The Bell, The

43

Nice and the Good, The Sandcastle, Under the Net,
The Unicorn]

435.   Berthoff, Warner.   Fictions and Events: Essays in
       Criticism and Literary History.   New York: E. P.
       Dutton & Co., Inc., 1971, pp. 118-54.   [The Red and
       the Green]

436.   Bradbury, Malcolm.   Possibilities: Essays on the
       State of the Novel.   London, Oxford, and New York:
       Oxford University Press, 1973, pp. 231-46.   [Under
       the Net]

437.   Bronzwaer, W. J. M.   Tense in the Novel: An In-
       vestigation of Some Potentialities of Linguistic Criti-
       cism.   Groningen, The Netherlands: Wolters-Noord-
       hoff, 1970, pp. 81-116.   [Chapter IV: "The Italian
       Girl: An Explication"]

438.   Burgess, Anthony.   The Novel Now: A Guide to Con-
       temporary Fiction.   New York: W. W. Norton &
       Company, Inc., 1967, pp. 124-27, 128, 131, 137,
       146.   [The Bell, The Italian Girl, The Red and the
       Green, A Severed Head, Under the Net, The Unicorn,
       An Unofficial Rose]

439.   Byatt, Antonia Susan.   Degrees of Freedom: The
       Novels of Iris Murdoch.   London: Chatto & Windus,
       Ltd., and New York: Barnes & Noble, 1956, 224p.
       Reviewed by Frank Baldanza in Wisconsin Studies in
       Contemporary Literature 8 (Summer 1967):454-58; by
       S. W. Dawson in Essays in Criticism 16 (1966):330-
       35; by James Hall in Modern Language Quarterly 27
       (1966):103-105; by Stephen Wall in Listener 74 (1965):
       208; and anonymously in Times Literary Supplement
       [London], 29 July 1965, p. 630.   [The Bell, The
       Flight from the Enchanter, The Sandcastle, A Severed
       Head, Under the Net, The Unicorn, An Unofficial
       Rose]

440.   Detweiler, Robert.   Iris Murdoch's "The Unicorn":
       Introduction and Commentary.   Preface by Lee A.
       Belford, gen. ed., Religious Dimensions in Literature.
       New York: The Seabury Press, 1969, 32p.   [Discus-
       sion of the religious themes and significance of The
       Unicorn, along with "The Sublime and the Beautiful
       Revisited" and "The Darkness of Practical Reason."]

441. Ford, Boris, ed. The Modern Age. Vol. 7 of A Guide to English Literature. Harmondsworth, Middlesex, England and Baltimore, Md.: Penguin Books, Ltd., 1961, p. 491. [On Murdoch's earlier novels.]

442. Fraser, George S. The Modern Writer and his World. London: Derek Verschoyle, 1953; Andre Deutsch Ltd., and Penguin Books, Ltd., rev. ed., 1964; and New York: Frederick A. Praeger, Inc., 1965, pp. 29, 175, 184-87. [On Murdoch's earlier novels.]

443. Fricker, Robert. Der Moderne Englische Roman. Göttingen: Vandenhoeck & Ruprecht, 2 Aufl., 1966, pp. 3, 196, 214, 221, 223-26, 227, 235, 239, 252. [The Bell, The Flight from the Enchanter, The Sandcastle, Under the Net]

444. Gerstenberger, Donna. Iris Murdoch. Irish Writers Series. Lewisburg, Pa.: Bucknell University Press, and London: Associated University Presses, 1975, 85p. [The Red and the Green]

445. Gindin, James. Postwar British Fiction: New Accents and Attitudes. Berkeley and Los Angeles: University of California Press, 1962, pp. 178-95. [A Severed Head]

446. Grigson, Geoffrey. The Contrary View: Glimpses of Fudge and Gold. London: Macmillan Press Ltd., and Totowa, N.J.: Rowman & Littlefield, Inc., 1974, pp. 30-33. [The Unicorn]

447. Hall, James. The Lunatic Giant in the Drawing Room: The British and American Novel Since 1930. Bloomington, Ind. and London: Indiana University Press, 1968, pp. 181-212. [The Bell, The Flight from the Enchanter, The Sandcastle, A Severed Head, Under the Net, The Unicorn, An Unofficial Rose]

448. Ivask, Ivar, and von Wilpert, Gero, eds. World Literature Since 1945. New York: Frederick Ungar Publishing Co., 1973, pp. 69, 107, 108-109. [The Bell, The Flight from the Enchanter, The Italian Girl, The Red and the Green, The Sandcastle, A Severed Head, Under the Net, The Unicorn]

449.   Karl, Frederick R.   A Reader's Guide to the Con-
        temporary English Novel.   New York: Farrar, Straus
        & Giroux, rev. ed., 1972, pp. 3, 260-65, 326, 338-
        42, 354, 355.   [The Bell, Bruno's Dream, A Fairly
        Honourable Defeat, The Flight from the Enchanter,
        The Italian Girl, The Nice and the Good, The Red and
        the Green, The Sandcastle, Sartre: Romantic Rationa-
        list, A Severed Head, "The Sublime and the Beautiful
        Revisited," The Time of the Angels, Under the Net,
        The Unicorn, An Unofficial Rose]

450.   Kostelanetz, Richard, ed.   On Contemporary Litera-
        ture.   New York: Avon Books, expanded ed., 1969
        [1st ed., 1964], pp. 468-72.   [The Bell, The Flight
        from the Enchanter, The Sandcastle, A Severed Head,
        Under the Net]

451.   Lanoire, Maurice.   Les Lorgnettes du Roman Anglais.
        Paris: Librairie Plon, 1959, p. 234.   [The Flight
        from the Enchanter]

452.   Lichtheim, George.   Collected Essays.   New York:
        Viking Press, 1973, pp. 486-89.   [Sartre: Romantic
        Rationalist]

453.   Lodge, David.   The Novelist at the Crossroads and
        Other Essays on Fiction and Criticism.   Ithaca, N.Y.:
        Cornell University Press, and London: Routledge &
        Kegan Paul Ltd., 1971, pp. 6, 7, 9.   [The Unicorn]

454.   Mehta, Ved.   Fly and the Bottle: Encounters with
        British Intellectuals.   Boston and Toronto: Little,
        Brown & Co., 1962, pp. 51-57.   [Conversation with
        Iris Murdoch on the relationship between existentialism
        and British philosophy.]

455.   Neill, S. Diana.   A Short History of the English Novel.
        London: Collier-Macmillan Ltd., and New York:
        Collier Books, new rev. ed., 1964, pp. 394, 401-403.
        [The Bell, The Flight from the Enchanter, The Sand-
        castle, A Severed Head, An Unofficial Rose]

456.   O'Connor, William Van.   The New University Wits and
        The End of Modernism.   With a Preface by Harry T.
        Moore.   Carbondale, Ill.:   Southern Illinois University
        Press, 1963, pp. 1, 53-74, 81.   [The Bell, The
        Flight from the Enchanter, The Sandcastle, A Severed
        Head, Under the Net]

457. Oppel, Horst, ed. Der Moderne Englische Roman: Interpretationen. Berlin: Erich Schmidt Verlag, 1965, pp. 344-58. [Under the Net]

458. Raban, Jonathan. The Technique of Modern Fiction: Essays in Practical Criticism. London: Edward Arnold, Ltd., 1968, and Notre Dame, Ind.: University of Notre Dame Press, 1969, pp. 10, 60, 69, 70, 104-111. [The Red and the Green, The Sandcastle, Under the Net]

459. Rabinovitz, Rubin. Iris Murdoch. Monograph-- Columbia Essays on Modern Writers, No. 34. New York and London: Columbia University Press, 1968, 48p. Reviewed by Josephine Z. Knopp in Modern Language Journal 53 (1969):132; by Larry L. Dickson in Abstracts of English Studies 15 (April 1972):521; and by H. T. Mason in Notes and Queries 17 (1970): 394-97. [The Bell, The Flight from the Enchanter, The Italian Girl, The Nice and the Good, The Red and the Green, The Sandcastle, A Severed Head, The Time of the Angels, Under the Net, The Unicorn, An Unofficial Rose]

460. Riley, Carolyn, and Harte, Barbara, eds. Contemporary Literary Criticism. Vol. 2. Excerpts from Criticism of the Works of Today's Novelists, Poets, Playwrights, and Other Creative Writers. Detroit: Gale Research Company, Book Tower, 1974, pp. 295-98. [Selections from the reviews of Murdoch's novels.]

461. Rippier, Joseph S. Some Postwar English Novelists. Frankfurt/Main: Diesterweg, 1965, pp. 71-103. [The Bell, The Flight from the Enchanter, The Sandcastle, A Severed Head, Under the Net, The Unicorn, An Unofficial Rose]

462. Robson, W. W. Modern English Literature. London, Oxford, and New York: Oxford University Press, 1970, p. 155. [Under the Net and Murdoch's novels in general]

463. Salem, James M. Drury's Guide to Best Plays. Metuchen, N.J.: The Scarecrow Press, Inc., 2nd ed., 1969, p. 281. [Brief description of A Severed Head]

464.   Shapiro, Charles, ed. Contemporary British Novelists.
        With a Preface by Harry T. Moore. Carbondale and
        Edwardsville, Ill.: Southern Illinois University Press,
        1965, pp. 62-80. [The Bell, The Flight from the En-
        chanter, The Italian Girl]

465.   Sheed, Wilfrid. The Morning After: Selected Essays
        and Reviews. With a Foreword by John Leonard.
        New York: Farrar, Straus & Giroux, and Toronto:
        Doubleday Canada Ltd., 1971, pp. 286-98. [The
        Italian Girl, The Red and the Green, A Severed Head]

466.   Stevenson, Lionel. The English Novel: A Panorama.
        Cambridge, Mass.: Riverside Press, 1960; Boston:
        Houghton Mifflin Co., 1960; and London: Constable,
        1961, p. 493. [Iris Murdoch is referred to as one
        of the "writers who take a more fastidious intellectual
        pose."]

467.   _____. The History of the English Novel. Vol.
        11. New York: Barnes & Noble, Inc., 1967, pp. 154,
        390-401, 405. [The Bell, The Flight from the En-
        chanter, The Italian Girl, The Red and the Green, The
        Sandcastle, A Severed Head, The Time of the Angels,
        Under the Net, The Unicorn, An Unofficial Rose]

468.   Swinden, Patrick. Unofficial Selves: Character in the
        Novel from Dickens to the Present Day. New York:
        Harper & Row, Publishers, Inc.; Barnes & Noble
        Book, 1973, pp. 82, 87, 118-19, 211-13, 221, 230-
        56, 257. ["Against Dryness," The Bell, Bruno's
        Dream, A Fairly Honourable Defeat, The Flight from
        the Enchanter, The Italian Girl, The Nice and the
        Good, A Severed Head, The Time of the Angels,
        Under the Net, The Unicorn, An Unofficial Rose]

469.   Temple, Ruth Z., and Tucker, Martin, eds. A Li-
        brary of Literary Criticism: Modern British Litera-
        ture. Vol. 2. New York: Frederick Ungar Publish-
        ing Co., 1966, pp. 351-54. [Selections from the re-
        views of Murdoch's novels.]

470.   West, Paul. The Modern Novel. London: Hutchin-
        son & Co., Ltd., 1963, pp. 126, 134, 144, 145.
        [The Bell, The Flight from the Enchanter, The Sand-
        castle, A Severed Head, Under the Net, An Unofficial
        Rose]

471.   Wolfe, Peter. The Disciplined Heart: Iris Murdoch
       and her Novels.   Columbia, Mo.: University of Mis-
       souri Press, 1966, 220p.   Reviewed by Frank Baldanza
       in South Atlantic Quarterly 66 (1967):634-35, and in
       Wisconsin Studies in Contemporary Literature 8 (Sum-
       mer 1967):454-58.   [The Bell, The Flight from the
       Enchanter, The Italian Girl, The Sandcastle, A Sev-
       ered Head, Under the Net, The Unicorn, An Unofficial
       Rose]

B. DISSERTATIONS

472. Anderson, Thayle Kermit. "Concepts of Love in the Novels of Iris Murdoch." Ph.D. dissertation. Purdue University, 1970. [Abstract in Dissertation Abstracts International 31 (April 1971):5385A-86A.]

473. Ashdown, Ellen Abernethy. "Form and Myth in Three Novels by Iris Murdoch: The Flight from the Enchanter, The Bell, and A Severed Head." Ph.D. dissertation. The University of Florida, 1974. [Abstract in Dissertation Abstracts International 35 (February 1975):5334A-35A.]

474. De Bens, Els. "A Study of the Works of Iris Murdoch." Licentiate thesis, University of Ghent, 1962.

475. Fast, Lawrence Edgar. "Self-Discovery in the Novels of Iris Murdoch." Ph.D. dissertation. University of Oregon, 1970. [Abstract in Dissertation Abstracts International 31 (April 1971):5397A.]

476. Gilligan, John T. "The Fiction and Philosophy of Iris Murdoch." Ph.D. dissertation. The University of Wisconsin--Milwaukee, 1973. [Abstract in Dissertation Abstracts International 35 (August 1974):1099A-100A.]

477. Goshgarian, Gary. "From Fable to Flesh: A Study of the Female Characters in the Novels of Iris Murdoch." Ph.D. dissertation. The University of Wisconsin, 1972. [Abstract in Dissertation Abstracts International 33 (January 1973):3583A.]

478. Kaplan, Morton Neil. "Iris Murdoch and the Gothic Tradition." Ph.D. dissertation. Columbia University, 1969. [Abstract in Dissertation Abstracts International 31 (September 1970):1231A-32A.]

479. Keates, Lois Silver. "Varieties of the Quest-Myth in

the Early Novels of Iris Murdoch." Ph. D. dissertation. University of Pennsylvania, 1972. [Abstract in
Dissertation Abstracts International 33 (October 1972):
1730A.]

480.   Rockefeller, Larry Jean. "Comedy and the Early
Novels of Iris Murdoch." Ph. D. dissertation. Bowl-
ing Green State University, 1968. [Abstract in Dissertation Abstracts 29 (May 1969):4018A.]

481.   Schneidermeyer, Wilma Faye. "The Religious Dimension in the Works of Iris Murdoch." Ph. D. dissertation. University of Southern California, 1974. [Ab-
stract in Dissertation Abstracts International 35 (November 1974): 3113A.]

482.   Stettler-Imfeld, Barbara. "The Adolescent in the
Novels of Iris Murdoch." Ph. D. dissertation. University of Bern, 1970.

483.   Stimpson, Catharine Roslyn. "The Early Novels of
Iris Murdoch." Ph. D. dissertation. Columbia University, 1967. [Abstract in Dissertation Abstracts
28 (June 1968):5073A-74A.]

484.   Stinson, John Jerome. "The Uses of the Grotesque
and Other Modes of Distortion: Philosophy and Impli-
cation in the Novels of Iris Murdoch, William Golding,
Anthony Burgess, and J. P. Donleavy." Ph. D. dissertation. New York University, 1971. [Abstract in
Dissertation Abstracts International 32 (September
1971):1533A.]

485.   Sullivan, Zohreh Tawakuli. "Enchantment and the
Demonic in the Novels of Iris Murdoch." Ph. D. dissertation. University of Illinois at Urbana-Champaign,
1970. [Abstract in Dissertation Abstracts International
32 (July 1971):458A.]

486.   Wolf, Nancy Connors. "Philosophical Ambivalence in
the Novels of Iris Murdoch." Ph. D. dissertation.
The University of Connecticut, 1972. [Abstract in
Dissertation Abstracts International 33 (December
1972):2959A.]

487.   Wolfe, Peter. "Philosophical Themes in the Novels
of Iris Murdoch." Ph. D. dissertation. The Univer-

sity of Wisconsin, 1965. [Abstract in Dissertation Abstracts 26 (December 1965):3357-58.]

C.   CRITICAL ESSAYS

488.   Anonymous.   "Altar to Evil. " Newsweek 68 (26 September 1966):118. [The Time of the Angels]

489.   _____. "An Arion Questionnaire: ʽThe Classics and the Man of Letters.ʼ" Arion 3 (Winter 1964):5-100. Also in Mother Mary Anthony, Abstracts of English Studies 9 (January 1966):2-3.

490.   _____. "Bad Spell in London. " Time 67 (14 May 1956):133-34. [The Flight from the Enchanter]

491.   _____. "Change of Life. " Economist 241 (6 November 1971):vi-vii. [An Accidental Man]

492.   _____. "Characters in Love. " Times Literary Supplement [London], 25 January 1968, p. 77. Also in T. L. S.: Essays and Reviews from Times Literary Supplement 1968, vol. 7, pp. 58-61. [No editor given.] London, New York, and Toronto: Oxford University Press, 1969. [The Nice and the Good]

493.   _____. "Circle of Hell. " Time 84 (11 September 1964):110. [The Italian Girl]

494.   _____. "Deep Mist and Shallow Water. " Time 81 (10 May 1963):104. [The Unicorn]

495.   _____. "The Donkeys. " Time 95 (9 March 1970): 69-70. [A Fairly Honourable Defeat]

496.   _____. "Enter Someone. " Times Literary Supplement [London], 10 September 1964, p. 837. [The Italian Girl]

497.   _____. "Fable Mates. " Times Literary Supplement [London], 6 September 1963, p. 669. Also in T. L. S.: Essays and Reviews from the Times Literary Supplement 1963, vol. 2, pp. 176-78. [No

53

editor given.] London, New York, and Toronto: Oxford University Press, 1964. [The Unicorn]

498. _____. "Fiction of 1968: Iris Murdoch: The Nice and the Good." In T. L. S.: Essays and Reviews from the Times Literary Supplement 1968, vol. 7, pp. 58-61. [No editor given.] London, New York, and Toronto: Oxford University Press, 1969.

499. _____. "Fiction of 1970: Iris Murdoch: A Fairly Honourable Defeat." In T. L. S.: Essays and Reviews from the Times Literary Supplement 1970, vol. 9, pp. 183-86. [No editor given.] London, New York, and Toronto: Oxford University Press, 1971.

500. _____. "Hanging by a Thread." Time 93 (21 February 1969):84-85, E7. [Bruno's Dream]

501. _____. "Hitlerian Parallels." Times Literary Supplement [London], 23 November 1973, p. 1418. ["The Three Arrows"]

502. _____. "Humor and Verse." Nation 178 (26 June 1954):548. [Under the Net]

503. _____. "I'll Move Mine If You Move Yours." Times Literary Supplement [London], 22 October 1971, p. 1305. [An Accidental Man]

504. _____. "In a Recognizable World." Times Literary Supplement [London], 22 March 1974, p. 281. [The Sacred and Profane Love Machine]

505. _____. "In the Heart or in the Head." Times Literary Supplement [London], 7 November 1958, p. 640. Also in John K. Mathison, Abstracts of English Studies 2 (August 1959):262. [The Bell]

506. _____. "Iris Murdoch Number." Modern Fiction Studies 15 (Autumn 1969):335-457.

507. _____. "Irish Stew." Newsweek 66 (22 November 1965):113A, 114. [The Red and the Green]

508. _____. "It Tolls, but for Whom?" Time 72 (27 October 1958):94. [The Bell]

509.   . "Ladies' Quintet." Books of the Month
[London], July 1961, p. 15. [A Severed Head]

510.   . "Leisured Philanderings." Times Literary
Supplement [London], 16 June 1961, p. 369.

511.   . "Letting Others Be." Times Literary
Supplement [London], 23 February 1973, p. 197. [The
Black Prince]

512.   . "Love in the Mind's Eye," Time 84 (6
November 1964):52. [A Severed Head]

513.   . "Novels of 1963: Iris Murdoch: The Uni-
corn." In T. L. S.: Essays and Reviews from the
Times Literary Supplement 1963, vol. 2, pp. 176-78.
[No editor given.] London, New York, and Toronto:
Oxford University Press, 1964.

514.   . "Novels of 1965: Iris Murdoch: The Red
and the Green." In T. L. S.: Essays and Reviews
from the Times Literary Supplement 1965, vol. 4,
pp. 40-41. [No editor given.] London, New York,
and Toronto: Oxford University Press, 1966.

515.   . "Novels of 1966: Iris Murdoch: The Time
of the Angels." In T. L. S.: Essays and Reviews from
the Times Literary Supplement 1966, vol. 5, pp. 33-36.
[No editor given.] London, New York, and Toronto:
Oxford University Press, 1967.

516.   . "Out of School." Times Literary Supplement [London], 10 May 1957, p. 285. [The Sand-
castle]

517.   . "Paying Attention." Times Literary Supplement [London], 26 February 1971, p. 241. [The
Sovereignty of Good]

518.   . "Perpetual Motion." Times Literary Supplement [London], 6 April 1956, p. 205. [The Flight
from the Enchanter]

519.   . "Philosophical Pixy." Time 69 (10 June
1957):106. [The Sandcastle]

520.   . "Picking Up the Pieces." Times Literary

Supplement [London], 8 September 1966, p. 798. Also
in T. L. S.: Essays and Reviews from the Times Literary Supplement 1966, vol. 5, pp. 33-36. [No editor
given.] London, New York, and Toronto: Oxford University Press, 1967. [The Time of the Angels]

521. _____ . "Republic and Private." Times Literary
Supplement [London], 14 October 1965, p. 912. Also
in T. L. S.: Essays and Reviews from the Times Literary Supplement 1965, vol. 4, pp. 40-41. [No editor
given.] London, New York, and Toronto: Oxford University Press, 1966. [The Red and the Green]

522. _____ . "Re-Run for the Enchanter." Times Literary Supplement [London], 29 January 1970, p. 101.
[A Fairly Honourable Defeat]

523. _____ . "Rich Bitches." Economist 246 (10 March
1973):118. [The Black Prince]

524. _____ . "Romantic Rationalist." Times Literary
Supplement [London], 15 January 1954, p. 45. [Sartre:
Romantic Rationalist]

525. _____ . "A Selection of the Year's Best Books."
Time 102 (31 December 1973):56. [The Black Prince]

526. _____ . "Short Notices." Time 77 (19 May 1961):
109-10. [A Severed Head]

527. _____ . "Soap Opera and Sensibility." Time 79
(25 May 1962):100-101. [An Unofficial Rose]

528. _____ . "Spiders and Flies." Times Literary Supplement [London], 16 January 1969, p. 53. [Bruno's
Dream]

529. _____ . "Stretching the Net." Times Literary Supplement [London], 8 June 1962, p. 425. [An Unofficial Rose]

530. _____ . "Town and Country." Times Literary Supplement [London], 9 July 1954, p. 437. [Under the
Net]

531. _____ . "Unbelievable Don." Time 86 (19 November 1965):LA 19. [The Red and the Green]

532. Ackroyd, Peter. "Iris Is No Pupil." Spectator 232
(23 March 1974):363-64. [The Sacred and Profane
Love Machine]

533. _____. "On the Top of the Word." Spectator 234
(26 April 1975):514 [A Word Child]

534. Ahlin, Lars; Gustafsson, Lars; and Ljungquist, Walter.
"Den Moderna Romanen." Bonniers Litterära Magasin
30 (April 1961):280-90.

535. Albérès, R. M. "Renaissance du Roman Picaresque."
Revue de Paris [vol. unknown] (February 1968):47:53.
Also in R. E. Wiehe, Abstracts of English Studies 13
(January 1970):267-77. ["Murdoch's novels ... show
that the novelistic imagination has been installed in
the picaresque."]

536. Allen, Walter. "Anything Goes." New York Times
Book Review, 25 September 1966, p. 5. [The Time
of the Angels]

537. _____. "The Surface Isn't All." New York Times
Book Review, 16 April 1961, p. 5. [A Severed Head]

538. Allott, Miriam. "The Novels of Iris Murdoch."
Talks to Teachers of English [Kings College, New-
castle-on-Tyne] no. 2 (1962):57-71.

539. Amis, Martin. "Alas, Poor Bradley." New Statesman 85 (23 February 1973):278-79. [The Black
Prince]

540. _____. "Queasy Rider." New Statesman 87 (22
March 1974):414. [The Sacred and Profane Love
Machine]

541. Arnaud, Pierre. "Les vertus du chiffre sept et le
mythe de la dame à la licorne. Essai d'interprétation
de The Unicorn, d'Iris Murdoch." Les Langues
Modernes 2 (1968):206-10.

542. Bailey, Paul. "Naming Love." Manchester Guardian
Weekly, 6 April 1974, p. 22. [The Sacred and Profane Love Machine]

543. Balakian, Nona. "Flight from Innocence." Books
Abroad 33 (Summer 1959):261, 268-70.

544. Baldanza, Frank. "Iris Murdoch and the Theory of
      Personality." Criticism 7 (Spring 1965):176-89.

545. _____. "The Murdoch Manuscripts at the Univer-
      sity of Iowa: An Addendum." Modern Fiction Studies
      16 (1970):201-202.

546. _____. "The Nice and the Good." Modern Fiction
      Studies 15 (Autumn 1969):417-28.

547. Barrett, William. "English Opposites." Atlantic
      Monthly 211 (June 1963):131-32. [The Unicorn]

548. _____. "Roses with Thorns." Atlantic Monthly
      209 (June 1962):108-109. [An Unofficial Rose]

549. Barrows, John. "Iris Murdoch." John O'London's
      4 (4 May 1961):498. Also in Lawrence R. Dawson,
      Jr., Abstracts of English Studies 4 (September 1961):
      379. [The Flight from the Enchanter, The Sand-
      castle, Under the Net]

550. Batchelor, Billie. "Revision in Iris Murdoch's Under
      the Net." Books at Iowa [University of Iowa] no. 8
      (April 1968):30-36. Also in Michael Masi, Abstracts
      of English Studies 15 (April 1972):521.

551. Bell, Pearl K. "In a Tangle of Crashing Symbols."
      Christian Science Monitor 27 January 1972, p. 10.
      [An Accidental Man]

552. Bergonzi, Bernard. "Nice but Not Good." New York
      Review of Books 10 (11 April 1968):36-38. [The Nice
      and the Good]

553. Beriger, Hanno. "Iris Murdoch: The Nice and the
      Good." Mitteilungen aus dem Freien Gymnasium
      Bern [Switzerland] no. 1 (June 1969):11-21.

554. Berthoff, Warner. "The Enemy of Freedom Is Fan-
      tasy." Massachusetts Review 8 (Summer 1967):580-
      84.

555. _____. "Fortunes of the Novel: Muriel Spark and
      Iris Murdoch." Massachusetts Review 8 (Spring 1967):
      301-32. Also in Warner Berthoff, Fictions and
      Events: Essays in Criticism and Literary History,

pp. 118-54. New York: E. P. Dutton & Co., Inc. 1971. And in Robert L. Dial, Abstracts of English Studies 12 (May 1969):249. [The Red and the Green]

556.   Betjeman, John. "Miss Murdoch's Lay Community." Publishers Weekly 189 (June 1966):129. [The Bell]

557.   Billington, Michael. "Novel into Play." Play and Players 15 (March 1968):26. [James Saunders talking to Michael Billington about the adaptation of Iris Murdoch's The Italian Girl into a play.]

558.   Blair, Howard. "The Legend of a Bell--and Three Frantic People." San Francisco Chronicle This World, 2 November 1958, p. 20. [The Bell]

559.   Bowen, Elizabeth. "Sensuality in a Secluded World." Saturday Review 41 (25 October 1958):24. [The Bell]

560.   Bowen, John. "One Man's Meat: The Idea of Individual Responsibility." Times Literary Supplement [London], 7 August 1959, pp. xii-xiii.

561.   . "One Must Say Something." New York Times Book Review. 7 November 1965, pp. 4-5. [The Red and the Green]

562.   Bradbury, Malcolm. "'A House Fit for Free Characters': Iris Murdoch and Under the Net." Critical Quarterly [Manchester, England] 4 (Spring 1962):47-54. Reprinted in Malcolm Bradbury, Possibilities: Essays on the State of the Novel, pp. 231-46. London, Oxford, and New York: Oxford University Press, 1973. Also in Sven Eric Molin, Abstracts of English Studies 5 (September 1962):303.

563.   . "The Romantic Miss Murdoch." Spectator 214 (3 September 1965):293. [The Red and the Green]

564.   . "Under the Symbol." Spectator, 6 September 1963, pp. 210-95. [The Unicorn]

565.   Bradley, Van Allen. "The Emotional Perils in Pathway of Love." San Francisco Chronicle, 29 August 1962, p. 39. [An Unofficial Rose]

566.   Breit, Harvey. "Enchanter." New York Times Book

Review, 22 April 1956, p. 8. [The Flight from the
Enchanter]

567. Brezianu, Andrei. "'Eşcul' lui Iris Murdoch." ["The
Defeat of Iris Murdoch."] România Literară [Bucha-
rest] 3 (December 1970):20.

568. Broich, Ulrich. "Tradition und Rebellion: Zur
Renaissance des pikaresken Romans in der englischen
Literatur der Gegenwart." Poetica 1 (April 1967):
214-29. Also in John Fludas, Abstracts of English
Studies 11 (January 1968):45. [Under the Net]

569. Broyard, Anatole. "Adding Quiddity to Oddity." New
York Times, 18 January 1972, p. 29. [An Accidental
Man]

570. Brugière, Bernard. "L'Univers Romanesque d'Iris
Murdoch." Mercure de France 352 (December 1964):
699-711.

571. Bryden, Ronald. "Living Dolls." Spectator 208 (8
June 1962):755-56. Also in Robert Yackshaw, Ab-
stracts of English Studies 5 (September 1962):354.
[An Unofficial Rose]

572. _____. "Phenomenon." Spectator 206 (16 June
1961):885. [A Severed Head]

573. Buckler, Ernest. "People Survive Somehow." New
York Times Book Review, 20 May 1962, p. 5. [An
Unofficial Rose]

574. Buenzod, Janine. "Quatre romans d'Iris Murdoch."
Tribune de Genève, 5 September 1959 [pages unknown].

575. Buitenhuis, Peter. "The Lady in the Castle." New
York Times Book Review, 12 May 1963, pp. 4, 24.
[The Unicorn]

576. Byatt, Antonia Susan. "Kiss and Make Up." New
Statesman 75 (26 January 1968):113. [The Nice and
the Good]

577. _____. "The Spider's Web." New Statesman 77
(17 January 1969):86. [Bruno's Dream]

578. Byron, Bill. "Symbol Clash." Spectator 221 (9

September 1968):326. [The Time of the Angels]

579. Casey, Florence. "Gothic Murk in Murdochland."
Christian Science Monitor, 25 November 1964, p. 17.
[The Italian Girl]

580. Chapman, John. "'A Severed Head' Tricky Comedy."
New York Theatre Critics' Reviews 25 (9 November
1964):178. [First performance at the Royale Theater,
New York, 28 October 1964.]

581. Clayre, Alasdair. "Common Cause: A Garden in the
Clearing." Times Literary Supplement [London], 7
August 1959, pp. xxx-xxxi. [The Bell]

582. Clemons, Walter. "Booby Traps." Newsweek 79
(24 January 1972):68, 72, 72A. [An Accidental Man]

583. _____. "Writers, Lovers, Killers." Newsweek
81 (18 June 1973):102, 103-104. [The Black Prince]

584. Coleman, John. "Sexual Permutations." Observer
Weekend Review [London], 11 September 1966, p. 27.
[The Time of the Angels]

585. Comino, Ioana. "Iris Murdoch." Contemporary Annual 42 (October 1969):9.

586. Connolly, Cyril. "The Nature of Love: Iris Murdoch's Musical Chairs." The Sunday Times [London],
18 June 1961, p. 27. [A Severed Head]

587. Cook, Eleanor. "Mythical Beasts." Canadian Forum
43 (August 1963):113-14. [The Unicorn]

588. Cooper, Susan. "Fiction: Vintage, Intricate Murdoch." Christian Science Monitor, 23 October 1974, p.
13. [The Sacred and Profane Love Machine]

589. Cosman, Max. "Priapean Japes." Commonweal 74
(9 June 1969):286-87. [A Severed Head]

590. Culley, Ann. "Theory and Practice: Characterization in the Novels of Iris Murdoch." Modern Fiction
Studies 15 (Autumn 1969):335-45.

591. Davenport, Guy. "Britannia in Negligee." National

Review 22 (24 March 1970):314-15. [A Fairly Honourable Defeat]

592.   . "Fruitfully Good, I'm Sure. " National Review 20 (9 April 1968):350. [The Nice and the Good]

593.   . "History with its Eyes Wide Open. " National Review 18 (29 November 1966):1227. [The Time of the Angels]

594.   . "Messages from the Lost. " National Review 18 (8 February 1966):119-20. [The Red and the Green]

595.   . "Tables of Transformation. " National Review 21 (11 February 1969):131-32. [Bruno's Dream]

596.   . "Turn the Other Face. " National Review 16 (3 November 1964):978-79. [The Italian Girl]

597.   Dawson, S. W. "New Scrutinies, I: Iris Murdoch or, Anyone for Incest. " The Human World 2 (1971):57-61.

598.   De Mott, Benjamin. "Dirty Words?" Hudson Review 18 (Spring 1965):31-44. Also in Barbara A. Paulson, Abstracts of English Studies 9 (January 1966):35. [Under the Net]

599.   Dent, Allan. "At the Play. " Punch 244 (22 May 1963):751. [Review of Theatre Royal production of A Severed Head in Bristol.]

600.   Derrick, Christopher. "The Burden of the World. " Tablet [London] 216 (23 June 1962):595-96. [An Unofficial Rose]

601.   . "The Moated Grange. " Tablet [London] 217 (14 September 1963):986-87. [The Unicorn]

602.   . "Truth on a Hill. " Tablet [London] 215 (24 June 1961):609-10. [A Severed Head]

603.   Dick, Bernard F. "The Novels of Iris Murdoch: A Formula for Enchantment. " Bucknell Review 14 (May 1966):66-81. Also in Michael M. Dorcy, Abstracts of English Studies 11 (April 1968):181. [Under the Net]

604.   Doherty, Paul C.   "The Year's Best Paperbacks. "
       America 130 (9 February 1974):93.   [A Fairly Honour-
       able Defeat]

605.   Donoghue, Denis.   "Magic Defeated. "   New York Re-
       view of Books 7 (17 November 1966):22-23.   [The
       Time of the Angels]

606.   Drabble, Margaret.   "Gothic Hollywood. "   Listener
       91 (17 January 1974):89.   [The Three Arrows and
       The Servants and the Snow]

607.   Drescher, Horst W.   "British Literature. "   In World
       Literature Since 1945, pp. 65-121.   Ed. by Ivar Ivask
       and Gero von Wilpert.   New York: Frederick Ungar
       Publishing Co. , 1973.   [Discussion of Murdoch's nov-
       els, pp. 107, 108.]

608.   Duchene, Ann.   "Funny Appalling. "   Manchester
       Guardian Weekly, 16 June 1961, p. 6.   [A Severed
       Head]

609.   Dzieduszychi, Michele.   "La Ragazza Irlandese. "   La
       Fiera Litteraria, 4 April 1968, p. 14.

610.   Eimerl, Sarel.   "Choreography of Despair. "   Reporter
       35 (3 November 1966):45-46.   [The Time of the An-
       gels]

611.   Emerson, Donald.   "Violence and Survival in the Nov-
       els of Iris Murdoch. "   Transactions of the Wisconsin
       Academy of Sciences, Arts, and Letters 57 (1969):21-
       28.

612.   Engelborghs, Maurits.   "Engelse Letteren: John
       Wain en Iris Murdoch. "   Dieste Warrande en Belfort
       [Antwerp] 58 (January 1958):50-56.

613.   F. , E. W.   "New Form for the Novel. "   Christian
       Science Monitor, 19 April 1956, p. 11.   [The Flight
       from the Enchanter]

614.   Felheim, Marvin.   "Symbolic Characterization in the
       Novels of Iris Murdoch. "   Texas Studies in Language
       and Literature 2 (Summer 1960):189-97.   Also in Wil-
       liam O. Harris, Abstracts of English Studies 4 (Jan-
       uary 1961):40.   [The Flight from the Enchanter, The
       Sandcastle]

615.   Fowlie, Wallace. "Figures from Two Tortured Gene-
        rations. " Commonweal 59 (13 November 1953):145.
        [Sartre: Romantic Rationalist]

616.   Fraser, George S. "Discussion of Iris Murdoch's
        Novels. " In George S. Fraser, The Modern Writer
        and His World, pp. 184-87. London: Andre Deutsch
        Ltd., rev. ed., 1954.

617.   _____. "Iris Murdoch: The Solidity of the Nor-
        mal. " International Literary Annual [London] 2 (1959):
        37-54. [The Sandcastle, Under the Net]

618.   Fraser, Kennedy. "Ordinary Human Jumble. " New
        Yorker 49 (30 July 1973):69-71. [The Black Prince]

619.   Fraser, R. A. "A Complicated Minuet of Love--in
        the English Manner. " San Francisco Chronicle This
        World, 30 April 1961, p. 27. [A Severed Head]

620.   Freedman, Richard. "Dialogue as Trenchant as a
        5-to-1 Martini. " Chicago Tribune Book World, 12
        January 1969, p. 3. [Bruno's Dream]

621.   Fremantle, Anne. "The Probable and the Possible. "
        Reporter 38 (25 January 1968):47-49. [The Nice and
        the Good]

622.   Fries, Udo. "Iris Murdoch: Under the Net. Ein
        Beitrag zur Erzähltechnik im Ich-Roman. " Die
        Neueren Sprachen 68 (September 1969):449-59. Also
        in K. P. S. Jochum, Abstracts of English Studies
        13 (January 1970):319.

623.   Fuller, Edmund. "Talented But Lazy. " New York
        Times Book Review, 20 June 1954, p. 15. [Under
        the Net]

624.   Furbank, P. N. "Gowned Mortality. " Encounter 23
        (November 1964):88-90. [The Italian Girl]

625.   Galloway, David D. "The Iris Problem. " Spectator
        215 (22 October 1965):520. [The Red and the Green]

626.   Gannett, Lewis. "At the Bottom of a Lake Was a
        Bell. " New York Herald Tribune Book Review, 16
        November 1958, p. 8. [The Bell]

627. Garis, Robert. "Playing Games." Commentary 43 (March 1967):97-100. [The Time of the Angels]

628. Gascoigne, Bamber. "Sex in the Head." Spectator 210 (17 May 1963):638. [A Severed Head]

629. Gellert, Roger. "Quaint Honor." New Statesman 65 (5 July 1963):24. [A Severed Head]

630. Gerard, Albert. "Lettres Anglaises: Iris Murdoch." Revue Nouvelle 39 (June 1964):633-40. Also in O. H. Rudzick, Abstracts of English Studies 9 (September 1966):462. [The Bell]

631. Gérman, Howard. "Allusions in the Early Novels of Iris Murdoch." Modern Fiction Studies 15 (Autumn 1969):361-77. [The Flight from the Enchanter, The Sandcastle, A Severed Head, Under the Net]

632. _____. "The Range of Allusions in the Novels of Iris Murdoch." Journal of Modern Literature 2 (1971): 57-85.

633. Gindin, James. "The Fable Begins to Break Down." Wisconsin Studies in Contemporary Literature 8 (Winter 1967):1-18. Also in Edward A. Kearns, Abstracts of English Studies 14 (October 1970):73. [Discussion of the fabulistic form in Murdoch's novels.]

634. _____. "Images of Illusion in the Work of Iris Murdoch." Texas Studies in Language and Literature 2 (Summer 1960):180-88. Also in James Gindin, Postwar British Fiction: New Accents and Attitudes, pp. 178-95. Berkeley and Los Angeles: University of California Press, 1962. And also in William O. Harris, Abstracts of English Studies 4 (January 1961): 40.

635. Goldberg, Gerald Jay. "The Search for the Artist in Some Recent British Fiction." South Atlantic Quarterly 62 (Summer 1963):387-401. Also in John M. Munro, Abstracts of English Studies 6 (October 1963): 469. [Murdoch's Under the Net is characterized as a paradigm case of the artist-hero of recent British fiction.]

636. Graham, A. R. "All Our Failures Are Failures of

Love. " New York Times Book Review, 26 October
1958, pp. 4-5. [The Bell]

637.   Graver, Lawrence. "A New Novel by Bradley Pearson
        (his last) in a New Novel by Iris Murdoch (one of her
        best). " New York Times Book Review, 3 June 1973,
        pp. 1, 12, 14. [The Black Prince]

638.   Gray, James. "Lost Enchantment. " Saturday Review
        40 (18 May 1957):41. [The Sandcastle]

639.   Green, Peter. "Bomb in a Bloomsbury Eden. " Daily
        Telegraph and Morning Post [London], 16 June 1961,
        p. 18. [A Severed Head]

640.   Gregor, Ian. "Towards a Christian Literary Criti-
        cism. " Month 33 (April 1965):239-49. [A Severed
        Head]

641.   Griffin, James. "The Fat Ego. " Essays in Criticism
        [Oxford] 22 (1972):74-83. [The Sovereignty of Good]

642.   Grigson, Geoffrey. "A Captured Unicorn. " In Geoffrey
        Grigson, The Contrary View: Glimpses of Fudge and
        Gold, pp. 30-33. London: Macmillan Press Ltd. , and
        Totowa, N. J. : Rowman & Littlefield, 1974.

643.   _____ . "Entre les Tombes. " New Statesman 66
        (13 September 1963):321-33. [The Unicorn]

644.   Halio, Jay L. "A Sense of the Present. " Southern
        Review 2 (Autumn 1966):952. [The Italian Girl, The
        Red and the Green]

645.   Hall, James. "Blurring the Will: The Growth of
        Iris Murdoch. " Journal of English Literary History
        [Johns Hopkins] 32 (June 1965):256-73. Also (ex-
        panded) in James Hall, The Lunatic Giant in the Draw-
        ing Room: The British and American Novel Since
        1930, pp. 181-82. Bloomington, Ind. and London:
        Indiana University Press, 1968. [The Bell, The
        Flight from the Enchanter, The Sandcastle, A Severed
        Head, Under the Net, The Unicorn, An Unofficial Rose]

646.   Hall, Roland. "British Books on Philosophy, 1962-
        1967. Part II. " British Book News no. 333 (May
        1968):321-26. Also in Frances K. Barasch, Abstracts

of English Studies 12 (January 1969):9. [Byatt, A. S. Degrees of Freedom: The Novels of Iris Murdoch]

647. Hall, William F. "Bruno's Dream: Technique and Meaning in the Novels of Iris Murdoch." Modern Fiction Studies 15 (Autumn 1969):429-43.

648. _____. "'The Third Way': The Novels of Iris Murdoch." Dalhousie Review 46 (Autumn 1966):306-18. Also in Morea Nalley, Abstracts of English Studies 11 (March 1968):125.

649. Hampshire, Stuart. "The Latest Hegelian." New Statesman and Nation 47 (2 January 1954):19. [Sartre: Romantic Rationalist]

650. Harrison, Barbara G. "Moral Checkmate." Saturday Review/World 2 (5 October 1974):24. [The Sacred and Profane Love Machine]

651. Hauerwas, Stanley. "The Significance of Vision: Toward an Aesthetic Ethic." Studies in Religion [Canadian journal] 2 (Summer 1972):36-49. [Critical analysis of Iris Murdoch's philosophy of ethics.]

652. Hebblethwaite, Peter. "Feuerbach's Ladder: Lessek Kolakowski and Iris Murdoch." Heythrop Journal 13 (April 1972):143-61.

653. _____. "Out Hunting Unicorns." Month 30 (October 1963):224-73. [The Unicorn]

654. Hewes, Henry. "The Eternal Hexagon." Saturday Review 47 (14 November 1964):53. [A Severed Head]

655. Hicks, Granville. "Acute Angles of a Triangle." Saturday Review 44 (22 April 1961):18. [A Severed Head]

656. _____. "By Love Possessed." Time 91 (5 January 1968):76, 79. [The Nice and the Good]

657. _____. "Easter Monday Insights." Saturday Review 48 (30 October 1965):41-42. [The Red and the Green]

658. _____. "Entrance to Enchantment." Saturday

<u>Review</u> 46 (1 May 1963):27-28. [The Unicorn]

659.   . "Hanging by a Thread. " <u>Saturday Review</u>
52 (18 January 1969):32. [Bruno's Dream]

660.   . "Literary Horizons. " <u>Saturday Review</u> 52
(18 January 1969):32. Also in Martha D. Rekrut, <u>Ab-</u>
<u>stracts of English Studies</u> 14 (June 1971):648. [Bruno's
Dream]

661.   . "Love Runs Rampant. " <u>Saturday Review</u>
51 (6 January 1968):27-28. [The Nice and the Good]

662.   . "The Operations of Love. " <u>Saturday Re-</u>
<u>view</u> 45 (19 May 1962):32. [The Bell, A Severed
Head, An Unofficial Rose]

663.   . "Rector for a Dead God. " <u>Saturday Re-</u>
<u>view</u> 49 (29 October 1966):25-26. [The Time of the
Angels]

664.   Hirsch, Foster. "Ruled by Some, Not Benign. " <u>Na-</u>
<u>tion</u> 215 (24 July 1972):59-60. [An Accidental Man]

665.   Hirukawa, Hisayasu. "Futatsu no Sukoron. " <u>Eigo</u>
<u>Seinen</u> [The Rising Generation] [Tokyo] 116 (1970):576-
77. [Two essays on the sublime--Burke and Murdoch.]

666.   Hobson, Harold. "Miss Murdoch's Unofficial Rose. "
<u>Christian Science Monitor,</u> 19 July 1962, p. 11.

667.   Hodgart, Patricia. "American Social Groups. " <u>Man-</u>
<u>chester Guardian Weekly,</u> 10 June 1954, p. 11. [Un-
der the Net]

668.   Hoffman, Frederick J. "Iris Murdoch: The Reality
of Persons. " <u>Critique: Studies in Modern Fiction</u> 7
(Spring 1964):48-57. [The Bell, The Flight from the
Enchanter, The Sandcastle, A Severed Head, Under
the Net, The Unicorn, An Unofficial Rose]

669.   . "The Miracle of Contingency: The Novels
of Iris Murdoch. " <u>Shenandoah</u> [Washington and Lee
University] 17 (Autumn 1965):49-56. Also in Lewis
B. Horne, <u>Abstracts of English Studies</u> 9 (October
1966):524. [The Italian Girl]

670.   Holzhauer, Jean. "A Palpable Romantic. " <u>Common-</u>

weal 60 (4 June 1954):228. [Under the Net]

671.   Hope, Francis. "The Novels of Iris Murdoch." London Magazine n. s. 1 (August 1961):84-87. Also in Contemporary Literature. Ed. by R. Kostelanetz. New York: Avon Books, expanded edition, 1969 [1st ed., 1964], pp. 468-72. [The Bell, The Flight from the Enchanter, The Sandcastle, A Severed Head, Under the Net]

672.   _____. "Really Necessary?" New Statesman 82 (22 October 1971):561. [An Accidental Man]

673.   _____. "Strange and Unnatural." Observer [London], 25 February 1973, p. 36. [The Black Prince]

674.   Hopkinson, Tom. "A Natural Novelist." Observer [London], 5 May 1957, p. 17. [The Sandcastle]

675.   Hoskins, Robert. "Iris Murdoch's Midsummer Nightmare." Twentieth Century Literature 18 (July 1972): 191-98.

676.   Howe, Irving. "Realities and Fictions." Partisan Review 26 (Winter 1959):132-33. [The Bell]

677.   Ivănescu, Mircia, introd. In Prins în Mreje [Under the Net], pp. 5-8. Bucharest: Univers, 1971.

678.   Ivaševa, V. "Ot Sartra k Platonu" ["From Sartre to Plato"]. Voprosy Literatury [Moscow] 13 (1969):134-55. [Existentialism in recent English literature, especially in the writings of Iris Murdoch.]

679.   _____. "Ot Džordž Eliot k Anglijskomu Romanu 60-x Godov." Voprosy Literatury [Moscow] 15 (1971): 98-119.

680.   Jacobson, Dan. "Farce, Totem, and Taboo." New Statesman 61 (16 June 1961):956-57. Also in R. E. Wiehe, Abstracts of English Studies 4 (November 1961):504. [A Severed Head]

681.   James, G. "The Reassertion of the Personal." Texas Quarterly 1 (1958):126-34.

682.   Janeway, Elizabeth. "But Nobody Understands."

70 Iris Murdoch

New York Times Book Review, 13 September 1964,
p. 5. [The Italian Girl]

683.   . "Everyone Is Involved." New York Times
Book Review, 14 January 1968, p. 4. [The Nice and
the Good]

684. Jones, Dorothy. "Love and Morality in Iris Murdoch's The Bell." Meanjin Quarterly 26 (March 1967):
85-90. Also in Theodore F. Simms, Abstracts of
English Studies 11 (April 1968):204.

685. Kaehele, Sharon, and German, Howard. "The Dis-
covery of Reality in Iris Murdoch's The Bell." Publications of the Modern Language Association of
America 82 (December 1967):554-63. Also in Phillips
G. Daries, Abstracts of English Studies 11 (February
1968):102-103.

686. Kalb, Bernard. "Three Comers." Saturday Review
38 (7 May 1955):22. [Kingsley Amis, Iris Murdoch,
and John Wain]

687. Kane, Patricia. "The Furnishings of a Marriage:
An Aspect of Characterization in Iris Murdoch's A
Severed Head." Notes on Contemporary Literature
2 (1972):4-5.

688. Karl, Frederick R. "The Novel as Moral Allegory:
The Fiction of William Golding, Iris Murdoch, Rex
Warner, and P. H. Newby." In F. R. Karl, A
Reader's Guide to the Contemporary English Novel,
pp. 254-73. New York: Farrar, Straus & Giroux,
rev. ed., 1972.

689.   . "Postscript: 1960-1970--Iris Murdoch."
In F. R. Karl, A Reader's Guide to the Contemporary
English Novel, pp. 338-43. New York: Farrar,
Straus & Giroux, rev. ed., 1972.

690. Kaufman, R. J. "The Progress of Iris Murdoch."
Nation 188 (21 March 1959):255-56. Also in T. O.
Mallory, Abstracts of English Studies 2 (June 1959):
184.

691. Kaye, H. "Delight and Instruction." New Republic
160 (8 February 1969):19-20. [Bruno's Dream]

692. Kemp, Peter. "The Flight Against Fantasy: Iris
      Murdoch's The Red and the Green. " Modern Fiction
      Studies 15 (Autumn 1969):403-15.

693. Kenney, Alice P. "The Mythic History of A Severed
      Head. " Modern Fiction Studies 15 (Autumn 1969):387-
      401.

694. Kenny, Anthony. "Luciferian Moralists. " Listener
      85 (7 January 1971):23. [The Sovereignty of Good]

695. Kermode, Frank. "The British Novel Lives. " At-
      lantic Monthly 230 (July 1972):85-88. [An Accidental
      Man]

696. _____. "Myth, Reality, and Fiction. " Listener
      68 (1962):311-13. [Murdoch, Greene, Wilson, et
      al.]

697. _____. "Novels of Iris Murdoch. " Spectator 201
      (7 November 1958):618. [The Bell, Under the Net]

698. Kiely, Benedict. "England and Ireland. " New York
      Times Book Review, 5 June 1966, p. 5. [The Red
      and the Green]

699. Kiely, Robert. "On the Subject of Love. " Nation
      196 (25 May 1963):447-48. [The Unicorn]

700. Kimber, John. "The Bell: Iris Murdoch. " Delta
      18 (Summer 1959):31-34.

701. Kitchin, Laurence. "The Zombie's Lair. " Listener
      74 (4 November 1965):701-702, 704. Also in David
      G. Osborne, Abstracts of English Studies 11 (Feb-
      ruary 1968):86. [The Bell]

702. Kogan, Pauline. "Beyond Solipsism to Irrationalism:
      A Study of Iris Murdoch's Novels. " Literature and
      Ideology [Montreal] 2 (1969):47-69.

703. Kostelanetz, Richard. "Postscript, 1964. " In On
      Contemporary Literature, p. 472. Ed. by Richard
      Kostelanetz. New York: Avon Books, 1964. [Brief
      comments on The Unicorn and An Unofficial Rose.]

704. Kriegel, Leonard. "Iris Murdoch: Everybody through

the Looking-Glass. " In Contemporary British Novelists, pp. 62-80. Ed. by Charles Shapiro. Carbondale and Edwardsville, Ill.: Southern Illinois University Press, 1965.

705. _____. "A Surrender of Symbols. " Nation 199
(9 November 1964):339. [The Italian Girl]

706. Kuehl, Linda. "Iris Murdoch: The Novelist as
Magician/The Magician as Artist. " Modern Fiction
Studies 15 (Autumn 1969):347-60.

707. Kuehn, Robert E. "Fiction Chronicle. " Wisconsin
Studies in Contemporary Literature 6 (1965):135-37.

708. Kuin, J. "Gabrek aan morele verantwoordelijkheid. "
Raam 54 (1969):58-62.

709. Leech, Anastasia. "Anyone's Devil. " Tablet [Lon-
don] 218 (10 October 1964):1144. [The Italian Girl]

710. _____. "Fiction and Fact. " Tablet [London] 220
(24 September 1966):1074. [The Time of the Angels]

711. Lehmann, John. "English Letters in the Doldrums?"
Texas Quarterly 4 (Autumn 1961):56-63. Also in
Robert C. Jones, Abstracts of English Studies 6 (February 1963):86. [Murdoch and some other contemporary British writers are the new faces whose "real
interests" seem to lie "in sociology, critical theory,
and discussion. "]

712. Lehmann-Haupt, Christopher. "Another Iris Murdoch
Machine. " New York Times, 19 September 1974,
p. 41. [The Sacred and Profane Love Machine]

713. Leisi, Ilse. "Iris Murdoch Romankunst. " Neue
Zürcher Zeitung, 10 March 1968 [pages unknown].

714. Lemon, Lee T. "All You Need Is What?" Prairie
Schooner 48 (Winter 1974-75):366-67. [The Sacred
and Profane Love Machine]

715. Lerman, Leo. "English Novelists. " Mademoiselle
45 (September 1957):167.

716. Lerner, Laurence. "Metaphysick. " Encounter 38

(June 1972):73-74. [An Accidental Man]

717.   Lichtheim, George. "Across the Channel." In G.
        Lichtheim, Collected Essays, pp. 486-89. New York:
        Viking Press, 1973.

718.   Lindman-Strafford, Kerstin. "Förtrollning och Fången-
        skap." Finsk Tidskrift 175-176 (1964):402-10. [On
        Iris Murdoch's novels.]

719.   Ljungquist, Walter. "Med anledning av Iris Murdoch's
        'Mot Torrheten.'" Bonniers Litterära Magasin 30
        (April 1961):289.

720.   Lodge, David. "The Novelist at the Crossroads." In
        D. Lodge, The Novelist at the Crossroads and Other
        Essays on Fiction and Criticism, pp. 6-7. Ithaca,
        N.Y.: Cornell University Press, 1971. [On Mur-
        doch's earlier novels.]

721.   . "Le roman contemporain en Angleterre."
        La Table Ronde 179 (December 1962):80-92.

722.   Lurie, Alison. "Wise-Women." New York Review of
        Books 20 (14 June 1973):18-19. [The Black Prince]

723.   McCabe, Bernard. "The Guises of Love," Common-
        weal 83 (3 December 1965):270-73. Also in Bernard
        Farragher, Abstracts of English Studies 10 (February
        1967):76.

724.   McCarthy, M. "Dualities in The Bell." Contempo-
        rary Review 213 (17 December 1968):313-17.

725.   McClain, John. "Sustained Punch Lacking." New
        York Theatre Critics' Reviews 25 (9 November 1964):
        177-78. ["A Severed Head" at The Royale Theater
        in New York.]

726.   McDowell, Frederick P. W. "The Devious Involutions
        of Human Character and Emotions: Reflections on
        Some Recent British Novels." Wisconsin Studies in
        Contemporary Literature 4 (Autumn 1963):352-59. [An
        Unofficial Rose]

727.   . "Time of Plenty: Recent British Novels."
        Contemporary Review 13 (Summer 1972):361-94.

74   Iris Murdoch

[Discussion of Murdoch's novels.]

728.   McGinnis, Robert M. "Murdoch's The Bell." Ex-
       plicator 28 (September 1969):1, 3.

729.   Maddocks, Melvin. "Iris Murdoch: Heartfelt Wit."
       Christian Science Monitor, 11 January 1968, p. 11.
       [The Nice and the Good]

730.   _____. "Little England." Time 99 (7 February
       1972):LA7, 86. [An Accidental Man]

731.   _____. "Miss Murdoch's Sandcastle." Christian
       Science Monitor, 16 May 1957, p. 13.

732.   _____. "Wild Minuet." Time 101 (18 June 1973):
       84. [The Black Prince]

733.   Maes-Jelinek, Hena. "A House for Free Characters:
       The Novels of Iris Murdoch." Revue des Langues
       Vivantes [Brussels] 29 (1963):45-69. [The Flight from
       the Enchanter, The Sandcastle, A Severed Head, Under
       the Net, An Unofficial Rose]

734.   Majdiak, Daniel. "Romanticism in the Aesthetics of
       Iris Murdoch." Texas Studies in Literature and Lan-
       guage 14 (1972):359-75.

735.   Malcolm, Donald. "To Everyone with Love." New
       Yorker 37 (6 May 1961):172-76. [A Severed Head]

736.   Mano, D. Keith. "Enormous Trifles." National Re-
       view 24 (14 April 1972):408-409. [An Accidental
       Man]

737.   Marsh, Pamela. "Lights in the Shadow." Christian
       Science Monitor, 23 January 1969, p. 11. [Bruno's
       Dream]

738.   Martin, Graham. "Iris Murdoch and the Symbolist
       Novel." British Journal of Aesthetics 5 (July 1965):
       296-300.

739.   Martz, Louis L. "Iris Murdoch: The London Novels."
       In Twentieth-Century Literature in Retrospect, pp. 65-
       86. Ed. by Reuben A. Brower. Cambridge, Mass.:
       Harvard University Press, 1971. [The Bell, Bruno's

Dream, A Fairly Honourable Defeat, The Flight from
the Enchanter, The Italian Girl, The Nice and the
Good, The Red and the Green, The Sandcastle, A
Severed Head, The Time of the Angels, Under the
Net, The Unicorn, An Unofficial Rose]

740. Meidner, Olga McDonald. "The Progress of Iris
Murdoch. " English Studies in Africa 4 (March 1961):
17-38. Also in S. J. Sackett, Abstracts of English
Studies 4 (September 1961):373. [The Bell, Under
the Net]

741. _____. "Reviewer's Bane: A Study of Iris Murdoch's Flight from the Enchanter. " Essays in Criticism [Oxford] 11 (October 1961):435-47. Also in
A. G. Newell, Abstracts of English Studies 5 (May
1962):207.

742. Micha, Rene. "Les Romans 'à Machines' d'Iris Murdoch. " Critique [Paris] 16 (April 1960):291-301.
Also in J. Max Patrick, Abstracts of English Studies
3 (November 1960):485.

743. Miller, Karl. "The Sisterhood. " New York Review
of Books 18 (20 April 1972):19-20. [An Accidental
Man]

744. Miller, Vincent. "Unofficial Roses. " National Review 13 (11 September 1962):194-96. Also in John O.
Waller, Abstracts of English Studies 6 (February
1963):71. [An Unofficial Rose]

745. Miner, Earl. "Iris Murdoch: The Uses of Love. "
Nation 194 (2 June 1962):489-99. [A Severed Head,
An Unofficial Rose]

746. Moody, Philippa. "In the Lavatory of the Athenaeum
--Post War English Novels. " Melbourne Critical Re-
view 6 (1963):83-92. Also in Carolann B. Purcell,
Abstracts of English Studies 7 (September 1964):355.
[A Severed Head]

747. Morrell, Roy. "Iris Murdoch: The Early Novels. "
Critical Quarterly [Manchester, England] 9 (Autumn
1967):272-82. Also in Fred Erisman, Abstracts of
English Studies 11 (June 1968):299.

748. Mortimer, Raymond. "Notable Novelist: Miss Iris

Murdoch's Three Books. " The Sunday Times [London], 5 May 1957, p. 6. [The Flight from the Enchanter, The Sandcastle, Under the Net]

749.   Murray, William M. "A Note on the Iris Murdoch Manuscripts in the University of Iowa Libraries. " Modern Fiction Studies 15 (Autumn 1969):445-48.

950.   Mutis, C. Guido. "El mundo arquetipico de Iris Murdoch: El viaje y el descenso al infierno en Flight from the Enchanter. " Estudios Filológicos 6 (1970): 229-89.

751.   Nadel, Norman. "'Severed Head' Is a Stunning New Comedy. " New York Theatre Critics' Reviews 25 (9 November 1964):180. ["A Severed Head" at The Royale Theater in New York.]

752.   Narita, Seiju. "Tokyo no Iris Murdoch. " Eigo Seinen [The Rising Generation] [Tokyo] 115 (1969), 218-19. [Murdoch's visit to Tokyo.]

753.   Natan, Alex. "Symbolik und moderne Psychologie in den Romanen von Iris Murdoch. " Tagesanzeiger [Zürich], 23 June 1962 [pages unknown].

754.   _____. "Symbolismus mit Struwwelkopf. " Frankfurter Allgemeine Zeitung, 27 November 1963 [pages unknown].

755.   Oates, Joyce Carol. "Diversions of a Literary Puppet-Mistress. " Chicago Tribune Book World, 1 February 1970, p. 4. [A Fairly Honourable Defeat]

756.   _____. "So Many People!" Chicago Tribune Book World, 23 January 1972, p. 3. [An Accidental Man]

757.   O'Connor, William Van. "Iris Murdoch: The Formal and the Contingent. " In W. V. O'Connor, The New University Wits and The End of Modernism, pp. 52-74. Preface by Harry T. Moore. Carbondale, Southern Illinois University Press, 1963. Also in Earl H. Rovit, Abstracts of English Studies 3 (October 1960):443. [The Bell, The Flight from the Enchanter, The Sandcastle, Under the Net]

758.   _____. "Iris Murdoch: A Severed Head. "

Critique: Studies in Modern Fiction 5 (Spring-Summer 1962):74-77. Also in W. V. O'Connor, The New University Wits and The End of Modernism, pp. 70-74. Preface by Harry T. Moore. Carbondale, Ill.: Southern Illinois University Press, 1963.

759. _____. "Two Types of 'Heroes' in Post-War British Fiction." Publications of the Modern Language Association of America 77 (March 1962):168-74. Also in Manfred O. Triesch, Abstracts of English Studies 8 (September 1965):415. [The novels of Iris Murdoch and some other British writers are significant examples of post-war British fiction which emphasizes action, instead of individual consciousness.]

760. Ostermann, Robert. "Drama Created for the Mind's Eye." National Observer, 13 July 1974, p. 19. [The Three Arrows and The Servants and the Snow]

761. _____. "Life Entangles, Imprisons a Writer in Search of Truth and a Masterpiece." National Observer, 21 July 1973, p. 25. [The Black Prince]

762. _____. "Miss Murdoch's Morality Play Ignites a Roaring Dramatic Blaze." National Observer, 17 October 1966, p. 23. [The Time of the Angels]

763. _____. "Religion Gets Its Lumps in An Accidental Man." National Observer, 12 February 1972, p. 23.

764. O'Sullivan, Kevin. "Iris Murdoch and the Image of Liberal Man." Yale Literary Magazine 131 (December 1962):27-36. [The Flight from the Enchanter, The Sandcastle]

765. Pagones, Dorrie. "Wanton Waifs and a Roman Woman." Saturday Review 47 (19 September 1964):48-49. [The Italian Girl]

766. Palmer, Tony. "Artistic Privilege." London Magazine 8 (May 1968):47-52. Also in Robert Yackshaw, Abstracts of English Studies 11 (December 1968):523. [The Nice and the Good]

767. Parrinder, Patrick. "Pastiche and After." Cambridge Review 89A (4 November 1967):65-66. Also in James W. Sire, Abstracts of English Studies 11

(December 1968):509. [Murdoch's novels are called "pastiche."]

768. Paulding, Gouverneur. "Are Women Necessary? A Witty and Intelligent Novel." New York Herald Tribune Book Review, 6 June 1954, p. 4. [Under the Net]

769. ______. "Even the Landscape Has Homicidal Properties." New York Herald Tribune Book Review, 19 May 1963, p. 3. [The Unicorn]

770. ______. "Laughter, Horror Together in this Dream-Like Novel." New York Herald Tribune Book Review, 29 April 1956, p. 6. [The Flight from the Enchanter]

771. Pearson, Gabriel. "Fearful Symmetry." Manchester Guardian Weekly, 3 May 1975, p. 22. [A Word Child]

772. ______. "Iris Murdoch and the Romantic Novel." New Left Review nos. 13-14 (January-April 1962):137-45. Also in Edward Ruhe, Abstracts of English Studies 6 (September 1963):364-65. ["Against Dryness," The Bell, A Severed Head]

773. Pendry, E. D. "William Golding and 'Mankind's Essential Illness.'" Moderna Sprak 55 (1961):1-7. Also in Mary D. Smith, Abstracts of English Studies 7 (November 1964):489. [Murdoch and Golding resemble their predecessors in their "desire to evaluate seriously the nature of man."]

774. Pérez-Minik, Domingo. "Amigos y amantes, la comedia y la metafisica de Iris Murdoch." Insula 26 (February 1971):6.

775. Perrott, Roy. "Miss Murdoch Rings the Bell." Manchester Guardian Weekly, 13 November 1958, p. 11. [The Bell]

776. Peterson, Jes. "Iris Murdoch." Dansk Udsyn 45 (1965):196-203.

777. Phelps, Gilbert. "The Novel Today." In The Modern Age, pp. 475-95. Ed. by Boris Ford. Vol. 7 of The Pelican Guide to English Literature. Harmondsworth, Middlesex, England; and Baltimore, Md.: Penguin

Books, Ltd., 1961. [The Bell, The Flight from the Enchanter, The Sandcastle, Under the Net]

778.   Pickrel, Paul. "Heading toward Postcivilization." Harper's Magazine 229 (October 1964):128-32.

779.   _____. "Mostly about Women." Harper's Magazine 226 (June 1963):107-108. [The Unicorn]

780.   Pippett, Aileen. "Moonshine and Asphodel." New York Times Book Review, 15 April 1956, p. 31. [The Flight from the Enchanter]

781.   _____. "The Women in the Case." New York Times Book Review, 12 May 1957, p. 4. [The Sandcastle]

782.   Poirier, Richard. "Biting the Hand that Reads You." Book Week 3 (14 November 1965):5, 21-24. [The Red and the Green]

783.   _____. "The Politics of Self-Parody." Partisan Review 35 (Summer 1968):339-53. Also in Barbara A. Paulson, Abstracts of English Studies 12 (May 1969): 257. [Murdoch is one of those novelists who "assert that literature is as trivial a put-on as life" if the status given to fiction is not intimately connected with the "a priori standards of life, reality, and history."]

784.   Pondrom, Cyrena N. "Iris Murdoch: An Existentialist?" Comparative Literature Studies [University of Illinois] 5 (December 1968):403-19. Also in E. Nelson James, Abstracts of English Studies 12 (May 1969): 231. [Although Murdoch agrees with the existentialists on the question of freedom, she differs from them in her concept of partial freedom due to certain unavoidable contingencies.]

785.   _____. "Iris Murdoch: The Unicorn." Critique: Studies in Modern Fiction 6 (Winter 1963-64):177-80.

786.   Poore, Charles. "Gods, Associate-Gods, and Sinners." New York Times, 4 January 1968, p. 35. [The Nice and the Good]

787.   _____. "The Lady Millicent and Her Quadriga." New York Times, 4 November 1965, p. 45. [The Red and the Green]

788.   . "The Walls Came Tumbling Down." New
York Times, 29 September 1966, p. 45. [The Time
of the Angels]

789.   Porter, Raymond J. "'Leitmotiv' in Iris Murdoch's
Under the Net." Modern Fiction Studies 15 (Autumn
1969):379-85.

790.   Price, Martin. "Reason and Its Alternatives: Some
Recent Fiction." Yale Review 58 (Spring 1969):464-74.

791.   . "The Self-Deceivers: Some Recent Fiction."
Yale Review 48 (December 1958):272-75. [The Bell]

792.   Price, R. G. G. "A Fitful Backward Glance." Punch
251 (28 December 1966):970. [The Time of the Angels]

793.   . "The Personal Art." Punch 251 (14 September 1966):415. [The Time of the Angels]

794.   Pritchard, William H. "Senses of Reality." Hudson
Review 23 (Spring 1970):162, 165-66. [A Fairly
Honourable Defeat]

795.   Pryce-Jones, Alan. "The 'Creative Waywardness' of
Iris Murdoch." New York Herald Tribune, 4 November 1965, p. 23. [The Red and the Green]

796.   Queneau, Raymond. "A World of Fantasy." Time
and Tide 42 (6 July 1961):1119. Also in Lawrence R.
Dawson, Jr., Abstracts of English Studies 4 (October
1961):470. [A Severed Head]

797.   Quigly, Isabel. "Miss Murdoch and Others." Tablet
[London] 209 (18 May 1957):472. [The Sandcastle]

798.   Quinton, Anthony, et al. "The New Novelists: An
Enquiry." London Magazine 5 (November 1958):13-31.

799.   Raban, Jonathan. "Character and Symbolism." In
J. Raban, The Technique of Modern Fiction: Essays
in Practical Criticism, pp. 108-11. London: Edward
Arnold, Ltd., 1968; and Notre Dame, Ind.: Univer-
sity of Notre Dame Press, 1969. [The Red and the
Green, The Sandcastle, Under the Net]

800.   . "Lullabies for a Sleeping Giant." En-

counter 43 (July 1974):73-75. [The Sacred and Profane Love Machine]

801.   _____. "On Losing the Rabbit." Encounter 40
(May 1973):80-85. [The Black Prince]

802.   Rabinovitz, Rubin. "Iris Murdoch's Thirteenth Novel,
About Evil." New York Times Book Review, 8 February 1970, pp. 1, 28. [A Fairly Honourable Defeat]

803.   Raven, Simon. "Good News from Hades." Observer
[London], 21 January 1968, p. 31. [The Nice and the
Good]

804.   Raymond, John. "The Unclassifiable Image." New
Statesman 56 (15 November 1958):697-98. Also in
R. E. Wiehe, Abstracts of English Studies 3 (July
1960):320. [The Bell]

805.   Raynor, Vivien. "Something Keeps One Reading."
Washington Post Book World, 17 June 1973, pp. 4-5.
[The Black Prince]

806.   Reynolds, Stanley. "Artful Anarchy." New Statesman 79 (30 January 1970):157. [A Fairly Honourable
Defeat]

807.   Ricks, Christopher. "Man Hunt." New York Review
of Books 14 (23 April 1970):37-39. [A Fairly Honourable Defeat]

808.   _____. "A Sort of Mystery Novel." New Statesman 70 (22 October 1965):604-605. Also in R. E.
Wiehe, Abstracts of English Studies 9 (October 1966):
515-16. [Review of The Red and the Green, together
with A. S. Byatt's Degrees of Freedom: The Novels
of Iris Murdoch.]

809.   Ridley, M. R. "A Schoolmaster Falls in Love."
Daily Telegraph and Morning Post [London], 10 May
1957, p. 12. [The Sandcastle]

810.   Riisøen, Helge. "Iris Murdoch og Eksistensialismen."
Samtiden 82 (December 1973):597-602. Also in Bjorn
J. Tysdahl, Abstracts of English Studies 17 (May
1974):494.

811.   Rolo, Charles. "Liaisons Dangereuses." Atlantic

Monthly 207 (May 1961):98-100. [A Severed Head]

812.   . "Potpourri." Atlantic Monthly 194 (July
1954):85. [Under the Net]

813. Rome, M. R. "A Respect for the Contingent: A
Study of Iris Murdoch's Novel The Red and the Green."
English Studies in Africa 14 (1971):87-98.

814. Ryan, Marjorie. "Iris Murdoch: An Unofficial Rose."
Critique: Studies in Modern Fiction 5 (Winter 1962-
63):117-21.

815. Sage, Lorna. "No Time for Perfection." Observer
[London], 20 April 1975, p. 30. [A Word Child]

816. Sale, Roger. "Provincial Champions and Grandmas-
ters." Hudson Review 17 (Winter 1964-65):608, 612-
13. [The Italian Girl]

817.   . "Winter's Tales." New York Review of
Books 21 (12 December 1974):18, 22. [The Sacred
and Profane Love Machine]

818. Salvesen, Christopher. "A Hieroglyph." New Statesman 68 (11 September 1964):365-66. [The Italian
Girl]

819. Saxton, Mark. "Ingenious and Bizarre Novel of Emo-
tional Ambushes in London." New York Herald
Tribune Book Review, 16 April 1961, p. 27. [A
Severed Head]

820. Sayre, Nora. "A Poet's Journal, a Strange Western,
a Novel of Quest, a Philosopher's Fantasy." New
York Times Book Review, 23 January 1972, p. 7.
[An Accidental Man]

821. Scholes, Robert. "Iris Murdoch's Unicorn." In
Robert Scholes, The Fabulators, pp. 106-32. New
York: Oxford University Press, 1967.

822. Schrickx, W. "Recente Engelse Romankunst: Iris
Murdoch." Die Vlaamse Gids 46 (August 1962):516-32.
Also in S. J. Sackett, Abstracts of English Studies 6
(June 1963):309. [The Bell, The Flight from the En-
chanter, The Sandcastle, Under the Net]

823. Scott-Kilvert, Ian. "English Fiction 1958-60, II." British Book News no. 248 (April 1961):237-44. Also in Charles A. Toase, Abstracts of English Studies 7 (June 1964):261. [Iris Murdoch, Kingsley Amis, John Wain, et al. represent a group of novelists who denounce "a whole complex of literary conventions."]

824. Seehase, Georg. "Kapitalische Entfremdung und Humanistische Integration. Bemerkungen zum englischen proletarischen Gegenwartsroman." Zeitschrift für Anglistik und Amerikanistik 15 (1967):383-400. Also in W. Erzgräber, Abstracts of English Studies 12 (January 1969):52. [Predominance of the theme of alienation in Murdoch's novels.]

825. Seymour-Smith, Martin. "Virtue Its Own Reward." Spectator 220 (26 January 1968):103-104. [The Sovereignty of Good over Other Concepts]

826. Sheed, Wilfrid. "Iris Murdoch: The Red and the Green." In W. Sheed, The Morning After: Selected Essays and Reviews, pp. 286-98. Foreword by John Leonard. New York: Farrar, Straus & Giroux, and Toronto: Doubleday Canada Ltd., 1971. [The Italian Girl, The Red and the Green, A Severed Head]

827. _____. "Making a Meal of Antipasto." Book Week 2 (13 September 1964):5, 12. [The Italian Girl]

828. _____. "Nursery Politics." Commonweal 81 (4 December 1964):354. [A Severed Head]

829. Shestakov, Dmitri. "Afterword to Russian Translation of An Unofficial Rose." Moscow: Progress, 1971 [pages unknown].

830. _____. "An Iris Murdoch Novel in Russian." Soviet Literature 7 (1966):169-75. Also in Robert F. Damm, Abstracts of English Studies 12 (February 1969):92. [Reactions of Murdoch's characters to unexpected and chaotic situations constitute a "grotesque analysis of the psychology of our time."]

831. Simon, Irene. "Some Recent English Novels." Revue des Langues Vivantes 25 (1959):229-30. [The Bell]

832. Sisk, John P. "Melodramatic Story and Novel of

Ideas." Commonweal 69 (7 November 1958):154-55.
[The Bell]

833.   . "A Sea Change." Commonweal 66 (31 May
1957):236-37. [The Sandcastle]

834.   . "Uncrystallized Matter." Commonweal 64
(11 May 1956):158-59. [The Flight from the En-
chanter]

835. Skorodenko, V. "Foreword to Russian Translation of
The Red and the Green." Moscow: Progress, 1968.

836. Skow, John. "Uncouples." Time 104 (23 September
1974):97-98. [The Sacred and Profane Love Machine]

837. Sokolov, Raymond A. "Fleshly Rococo." Newsweek
71 (15 January 1968):73. [The Nice and the Good]

838. Souvage, Jacques. "The Novels of Iris Murdoch."
Studia Germanica Gandensia 4 (1962):225-52. Reviewed by K. H. Goller in Anglia 83 (1965):89-90.
[The Bell, The Flight from the Enchanter, The Sandcastle, The Time of the Angels]

839.   . "Symbol as Narrative Device: An Inter-
pretation of Iris Murdoch's The Bell." English
Studies 43 (April 1962):81-96. Also in Nils Eric
Enkvist, Abstracts of English Studies 5 (September
1962):319-20.

840.   . "Theme and Structure in Iris Murdoch's
The Flight from the Enchanter." Spieghel Historiael
van de Bond van Gentste Germanisten 3 (1960-61):
73-78.

841.   . "The Unresolved Tension: An Interpreta-
tion of Iris Murdoch's Under the Net." Revue des
Langues Vivantes [Brussels] 26 (1960):420-30. Also
in John S. Phillipson, Abstracts of English Studies
9 (September 1966):457.

842. Spacks, Patricia Meyer. "New Novels: In the
Dumps." Yale Review 64 (June 1975):590-92. [The
Sacred and Profane Love Machine]

843. Spurling, Hilary. "True Romance." Spectator 220

(16 February 1968):207. ["The Italian Girl" at Wyndham's Theatre in London.]

844. Straumann, Ursula. "Zwischen Phantasie und Kalkul, zum Romanwerk von Iris Murdoch." Die literarische Tat [Zürich], 9 March 1968 [pages unknown].

845. Swinden, Patrick. "Plots." In P. Swinden, Unofficial Selves, pp. 203-58. London: Macmillan and Company, Ltd., 1973.

846. Taubman, Howard. "Theater: Minuet of Marital Affections." New York Theatre Critics' Reviews 25 (9 November 1964):179-80. ["A Severed Head" at The Royale Theater in New York.]

847. Taubman, Robert. "L'Année Dernière at Dungeness." New Statesman 63 (8 June 1962):836. Also in R. E. Wiehe, Abstracts of English Studies 5 (December 1962):550-51. [An Unofficial Rose]

848. _____. "Not Caring." Listener 79 (1 February 1968):148. [The Nice and the Good]

849. _____. "Uncle's War." New Statesman 72 (16 September 1966):401-402. [The Red and the Green]

850. Taylor, Griffin. "What Doth it Profit a Man ... ?" Sewanee Review 66 (January-March 1958):137-41. [The Sandcastle]

851. Thomas, Edward. "Veteran Propellors." London Magazine 10 (April 1970):100-103. [A Fairly Honourable Defeat]

852. Thompson, John. "Old Friends." Commentary 45 (January 1968):65-67. [The Nice and the Good]

853. _____. "Plot, Character, Etc." Partisan Review 5-6 (1961):707-16. [The Flight from the Enchanter, A Severed Head]

854. Thomson, P. W. "Iris Murdoch's Honest Puppetry-- The Characters of Bruno's Dream." Critical Quarterly [Manchester, England] 11 (Autumn 1969):277-83. Also in Fred Erisman, Abstracts of English Studies 13 (March 1970):440-41.

855.   Thwaite, Anthony. "Chapters of Accidents." Observer [London], 24 March 1974, p. 39. [The Sacred and Profane Love Machine]

856.   Toynbee, Philip. "Miss Murdoch's Monster Rally." New Republic 155 (22 October 1966):24. [The Time of the Angels]

857.   _____. "Too Fruity to Be True." Observer [London], 18 June 1961, p. 28. [A Severed Head]

858.   Tracy, Honor. "Misgivings about Miss Murdoch." New Republic 151 (10 October 1964):21-22. [The Italian Girl]

859.   _____. "Passion in the Groves of Academe." New Republic 136 (10 June 1957):17. [The Sandcastle]

860.   Trevor, William. "Snobbery, Fun, Sex, and Sex." Manchester Guardian Weekly, 1 February 1968, p. 12. [The Nice and the Good]

861.   Trotzig, Birgitta. "Den Moderna Romanen." Bonniers Litterära Magasin 30 (May-June 1961):369-70.

862.   Tube, Henry. "Women's Rites." Spectator 222 (17 January 1969):79-80. [Bruno's Dream]

863.   Tucker, Martin. "Love and Freedom: Golden and Hard Words." Commonweal 77 (21 June 1963):357-58. [The Unicorn]

864.   _____. "More Iris Murdoch." Commonweal 81 (30 October 1964):173-74. [The Italian Girl]

865.   _____. "The Old Fish in Iris Murdoch's Kettle." New Republic 154 (5 February 1966):26-28. Also in William H. Magee, Abstracts of English Studies 9 (September 1966):449. [The Red and the Green]

866.   Updike, John. "Topnotch Witcheries." New Yorker 50 (6 January 1975):76-81. [The Sacred and Profane Love Machine]

867.   Vaizey, John. "A Sense of Doom." Listener 91 (21 March 1974):379-80. [The Sacred and Profane Love Machine]

868.   Vickery, John B.   "The Dilemmas of Language:
         Sartre's La Nausée and Iris Murdoch's Under the
         Net."   Journal of Narrative Technique 1 (May 1971):
         69-76.   Also in Priscilla M. Piché, Abstracts of
         English Studies 15 (March 1972):446.

869.   Viebock, Helmut.   "Iris Murdoch: Under the Net."
         In Der Moderne Englische Roman: Interpretationen,
         pp. 344-58. Ed. by Horst Oppel.   Berlin: Erich
         Schmidt Verlag, 1965.

870.   Vizioli, Paulo.   "O Romance de Iris Murdoch."   O
         Estado de São Paulo, Suplemento Literário, 28 Jan-
         uary 1967, p. 3.

871.   Voiles, Jane.   "A Third Murdoch Novel Comes as a
         Surprise."   San Francisco Chronicle, 10 May 1957,
         p. 19. [The Sandcastle]

872.   Wain, John.   "Iris Murdoch Novel about One Man and
         Two Women."   New York Times Book Review, 22
         September 1974, pp. 1-2.   [The Sacred and Profane
         Love Machine]

873.   _____ .   "Women's Work."   New York Review of
         Books 12 (24 April 1969):38-40.   [Bruno's Dream]

874.   Walker, Peregrine.   "Unlikely Quintet."   Tablet [Lon-
         don] 219 (30 October 1965):1213-14.   [The Red and
         the Green]

875.   Wall, Stephen.   "The Bell in The Bell."   Essays in
         Criticism [Oxford] 13 (July 1963):265-73.   Also in
         A. G. Newell, Abstracts of English Studies 6 (Novem-
         ber 1963):502.

876.   Wardle, Irving.   "A Dublin Romance."   Observer
         Weekend Review [London], 17 October 1965, p. 28.
         [The Red and the Green]

877.   Warnock, G. J.   "The Moralists: Values and
         Choices."   Encounter 36 (April 1971):81-84.   [The
         Sovereignty of Good]

878.   Warnock, Mary.   "Inner Circles."   New Statesman
         89 (18 April 1975):519-20.   [A Word Child]

879.   Wasson, Richard.   "Notes on a New Sensibility."

Partisan Review 36 (1969):460-77. Also in Barbara
A. Paulson, Abstracts of English Studies 14 (January
1971):281.

880.   Watrin, Jany. "Irish Murdoch's A Fairly Honourable
Defeat. " Revue des Langues Vivantes [Brussels] 38
(1972):46-64.

881.   Watts, Richard, Jr. "Witty British Rigadoon of Sex. "
New York Theatre Critics' Reviews 25 (9 November
1964):179. [Performance of "A Severed Head" at The
Royale Theater in New York.]

882.   Waugh, Auberon. "A Source of Wonder and Delight. "
Spectator 230 (24 February 1973):235-36. [The Black
Prince]

883.   Weatherhead, A. K. "Backgrounds with Figures in
Iris Murdoch. " Texas Studies in Literature and
Language 10 (Winter 1969):635-48.

884.   Webster, Harvey Curtis. "Grasp of Absurdity. "
Saturday Review 3 (3 July 1954):15. [Under the Net]

885.   Weeks, Edward. "Easter 1916. " Atlantic Monthly
216 (December 1965):138. [The Red and the Green]

886.   _____ . "Nice Is Not Always Safe. " Atlantic
Monthly 221 (February 1968):135-36. [The Nice and
the Good]

887.   _____ . "Satan in a Fog. " Atlantic Monthly 218
(October 1966):138, 140. [The Time of the Angels]

888.   Weightman, John. "Jean-Paul Sartre. " In The Novelist as Philosopher, pp. 102-27. Ed. by John
Cruickshank. London, New York, and Toronto: Oxford University Press, 1962. [Sartre: Romantic Ra-
tionalist]

889.   West, Paul. "O Tempora, O Mores. " Book Week 4
(25 September 1966):18. [The Time of the Angels]

890.   Whitehorn, Katharine. "Three Women. " Encounter
21 (December 1963):78-82. [The Unicorn] [Mary Mc-
Carthy, Muriel Spark, and Iris Murdoch]

891.   Whiteside, George. "The Novels of Iris Murdoch. "

Critique: Studies in Modern Fiction 7 (Spring 1964): 27-47. Also in D. Murray, Abstracts of English Studies 7 (October 1964):407-408. [The Bell, The Flight from the Enchanter, The Sandcastle, A Severed Head, Under the Net, The Unicorn, An Unofficial Rose]

892. Widmann, R. L. "Murdoch's Under the Net: Theory and Practice in Fiction." Critique: Studies in Modern Fiction 10 (1967):5-16. Also in Mary A. Grellner, Abstracts of English Studies 16 (June 1973):654.

893. Wilson, Angus. "Who Cares?" Manchester Guardian Weekly, 8 June 1962, p. 6. [An Unofficial Rose]

894. Zimmerman, Paul D. "Poor Fools." Newsweek 75 (16 February 1970):100. [A Fairly Honourable Defeat]

D. INTERVIEWS

895.   Barrows, John. "Living Writers--7: Iris Murdoch. "
John O²London's 4 (4 May 1961):498.

896.   Bryden, Ronald. "Talking to Iris Murdoch. " Listener
79 (4 April 1968):433-34. Also in David G. Osborne,
Abstracts of English Studies 13 (October 1969):108.

897.   Heyd, Ruth. "An Interview with Iris Murdoch. " University of Windsor Review [Windsor, Ontario] 1 Spring
1965):138-43.

898.   Hobson, Harold. "Lunch with Iris Murdoch. " The
Sunday Times [London], 11 March 1962, p. 28.

899.   Kermode, Frank. "House of Fiction: Interviews
with Seven English Novelists. " Partisan Review 30
(Spring 1963):62-82. Also in Barbara A. Paulson,
Abstracts of English Studies 7 (February 1964):82.
[Kermode discusses the relationship between fiction
and reality with Iris Murdoch, et al.]

900.   Mehta, Ved. "Onward and Upward with the Arts: A
Battle against the Bewitchment of our Intelligence. "
New Yorker 37 (9 December 1961):59-159.

901.   Nettell, Stephanie. "An Exclusive Interview. " Books
and Bookmen 11 (September 1966):14-15, 66.

902.   Rose, W. K. "An Interview with Iris Murdoch. "
Shenandoah [Washington and Lee University] 19 (Winter
1968):3-22. The same interview was published under
the title "Iris Murdoch, Informally, " London Magazine
8 (June 1968):59-73. Also in Lewis B. Horne, Abstracts of English Studies 11 (November 1968):497.

903.   Sale, Richard B. "An Interview in New York with
Walter Allen. " Studies in the Novel 3 (Winter 1971):
405-29. Also in William H. Magee, Abstracts of

English Studies 16 (January 1973):320. [Iris Murdoch, et al. are characterized as writers whose novels continue the comic tradition in English fiction and take comedy as being more serious than tragedy.]

E. BIOGRAPHIES

904.   Anonymous.   The Author's and Writer's Who's Who.
[No editor given.]   London: Burke's Peerage Ltd.,
5th ed., 1963, p. 354 and 1971, p. 581.

905.   _____. Contemporary Authors. Ed. by James
M. Ethridge and Barbara Kopala. Detroit: Gale
Research Company, The Book Tower, 1965, pp. 315-
16.

906.   _____. Current Biography Yearbook. Ed. by
Marjorie D. Candee. New York: H. W. Wilson Company, 1958, pp. 293-94.

907.   _____. The International Who's Who 1964-1974.
[No editor given.]   London: Europa Publications Ltd.,
1964, p. 773; 1965, p. 806; 1966, p. 866; 1967, p.
928; 1968, p. 942; 1969, p. 1062; 1970, p. 1138;
1971, p. 1164; 1972, p. 1188; 1973, p. 1200.

908.   _____. "The Observer Profile: Iris Murdoch."
Observer Weekend Review [London], 17 June 1962,
p. 23.

909.   _____. The Reader's Encyclopedia. Ed. by
William Rose Benét. London: Charles Black, 1965,
p. 694.

910.   _____. Two Hundred Contemporary Authors. Ed.
by Barbara Harte and Carolyn Riley. Detroit: Gale
Research Company, The Book Tower, 1969, p. 196.

911.   _____. Who's Who 1958. [No editor given.]
London: Adam & Charles Black, 1958, p. 2177.

912.   _____. Who's Who 1959. [No editor given.]
London: Adam & Charles Black, 1959, p. 2189.

913.   . Who's Who 1960, Who's Who 1961, Who's
Who 1962, Who's Who 1963, Who's Who 1964. [No
editor given] London: Adam & Charles Black, 1960,
p. 2170; 1961, p. 2185. London: Adam & Charles
Black and New York: St. Martin's Press, 1962, p.
2201; 1963, p. 2194; 1964, p. 2190.

914.   . Who's Who 1965, Who's Who 1966. [No
editor given.] London: Adam & Charles Black and
New York: St. Martin's Press, 1965, p. 2205; 1966,
p. 2206.

915.   . Who's Who 1967-1968 [through 1974-75].
[No editor given.] New York: St. Martin's Press,
1967, p. 2204; 1968, p. 2209; 1969, p. 2229; 1970, p.
2239; 1971, pp. 2265-66; 1972, p. 2301; 1973, p.
2329; 1974, p. 2364.

916.   . Who's Who 1975. [No editor given.] London: Adam & Charles Black, 1975, p. 2277.

917.   . Who's Who in the World 1971-1972, Who's
Who in the World 1974-1975. [No editor given.]
Chicago: Marquis Who's Who, Inc., 1st ed., 1970,
p. 664; 2nd ed., 1973, pp. 702-703.

918.   . The Writers Directory 1971-73. Ed. by
A. G. Seaton. Chicago and London: St. James
Press, 1971, p. 310.

919.   . The Writers Directory 1974-76. [No editor
given.] London: St. James Press and New York: St.
Martin's Press, 1973, p. 576.

920. Aitken, W. R. In Cassell's Encyclopedia of World
Literature, vol. 3, p. 207. Ed. by S. H. Steinberg.
New York: William Morrow & Company, Inc., 1973.

921. Baker, Roger. "Iris Murdoch." In Contemporary
Dramatists, p. 561. Ed. by James Vinson. Preface
by Ruby Cohn. London: St. James Press and New
York: St. Martin's Press, 1973.

922. Barrows, John. "Living Writers--7: Iris Murdoch."
John O'London's 4 (4 May 1961):498.

923. Borklund, Elmer. "(Jean) Iris Murdoch." In

Contemporary Novelists, pp. 911-15. Ed. by James
Vinson.   Preface by Walter Allen. New York: St.
Martin's Press, 1972.

924.   Breit, Harvey. "Enchanter." New York Times Book
Review 7 (22 April 1956):8.

925.   Colby, Vineta. "Biographical Sketch." Wilson Library Bulletin 33 (December 1958):268.

926.   Comino, Ioana. "Iris Murdoch." Contemporary Annual 42 (October 1969):9.

927.   Gindin, James. "Iris Murdoch." In J. Gindin, Post-
war British Fiction: New Accents and Attitudes, p.
242. Berkeley and Los Angeles: University of California Press, 1962.

928.   Hoffman, Frederick J. "Iris Murdoch." Encyclopedia
of World Literature in the 20th Century, vol. 2, pp.
431-32. Gen. ed. Wolfgang B. Fleischmann. New
York: Frederick Ungar Publishing Company, Inc.,
1969.

929.   O'Connor, William Van. "Iris Murdoch: The Formal
and the Contingent." In W. V. O'Connor, The New
University Wits and The End of Modernism, p. 55.
Preface by Harry T. Moore. Carbondale, Ill.:
Southern Illinois University Press, 1963.

930.   Osborne, Charles. "Murdoch, Iris (1919-   ) .... "
In The Penguin Companion to English Literature,
pp. 383-84. Ed. by David Daiches. New York:
McGraw-Hill Book Co., 1971.

F. BIBLIOGRAPHIES

931. Anonymous. Twentieth Century British Literature: A Reference Guide and Bibliography. Ed. by Ruth Z. Temple. New York: Frederick Ungar Publishing Company, 1968, p. 210.

932. Adelman, Irving, and Dworkin, Rita. The Contemporary Novel: A Checklist of Critical Literature on the British and American Novel Since 1945. Metuchen, N. J.: The Scarecrow Press, Inc., 1972, pp. 376-85.

933. Baker, Roger. "Iris Murdoch." In Contemporary Dramatists, pp. 562-63. Ed. by James Vinson. Preface by Ruby Cohn. London: St. James Press and New York: St. Martin's Press, 1973.

934. Baldanza, Frank. "Selected Bibliography." In Frank Baldanza, Iris Murdoch, pp. 179-84. New York: Twayne Publishers, Inc., 1974.

935. Civin, Laraine. "Iris Murdoch: A Bibliography." Johannesburg, South Africa: University of the Witwatersrand, 1968, 23p. [A Bibliography compiled in partial fulfillment of the requirements for the Diploma in Librarianship, Department of Bibliography, Librarianship and Typography, University of the Witwatersrand. Available in the Library of Congress, Washington, D. C.]

936. Culley, Ann, and Feaster, John. "Criticism of Iris Murdoch: A Selected Checklist." Modern Fiction Studies 15 (Autumn 1969):449-57.

937. Gerstenberger, Donna. "Selected Bibliography." In Donna Gerstenberger, Iris Murdoch, pp. 80-85. Lewisburg, Pa.: Bucknell University Press, and London: Associated University Presses, Irish Writers Series, 1975.

95

938.   Karl, Frederick R. "The Novel as Moral Allegory:
        The Fiction of William Golding, Iris Murdoch, Rex
        Warner, and P. H. Newby. " In Frederick R. Karl,
        The Contemporary English Novel, pp. 254-73. [On
        Iris Murdoch, pp. 260-65.] New York: Farrar,
        Straus & Cudahy, 1962. Also in Frederick R. Karl,
        A Reader's Guide to the Contemporary English Novel,
        pp. 3, 260-65, 326, 338-42, 354-55. New York:
        Farrar, Straus & Giroux, rev. ed., 1972.

939.   Mellown, Elgin W. "Murdoch, Jean Iris (1919-   )."
        In A Descriptive Catalogue of the Bibliographies of
        20th Century British Writers, pp. 264-66. Comp. by
        Elgin W. Mellown. Troy, N. Y. : Whitson Publishing
        Co. , 1972. [Brief checklist of some bibliographic
        references.]

940.   Murray, William M. "A Note on the Iris Murdoch
        Manuscripts in the University of Iowa Libraries. "
        Modern Fiction Studies 15 (Autumn 1969):445-48.

941.   Palmer, Helen H. , and Dyson, Anne Jane. "Bibliog-
        raphy of the Novels of Iris Murdoch. " In English
        Novel Explicator: Criticisms to 1972, pp. 211-19.
        Camden, Conn. : The Shoe String Press, Inc. , 1973.

942.   Schneidermeyer, Wilma. "The Religious Dimension
        in the Works of Iris Murdoch. " Ph. D. dissertation.
        University of Southern California, 1974, pp. 195-99.

943.   Stettler-Imfeld, Barbara. "The Adolescent in the
        Novels of Iris Murdoch. " An inaugural dissertation
        submitted to attain the Doctorate in the Faculty of
        Philosophy and History of the University of Bern,
        Switzerland. Zurich: Juris Druck, 1970, pp. 151-
        58. [The distinguishing feature of this bibliography
        is the inclusion of references to critical reviews, in
        French and German, of Iris Murdoch's novels.]

944.   Temple, Ruth Z. , and Tucker, Martin, comps. and
        eds. Twentieth Century British Literature: A Ref-
        erence Guide and Bibliography. New York: Frederick
        Ungar Publishing Co. , 1968, pp. 21, 59, 90, 91, 102.
        [Checklist of studies done on Murdoch and her novels.]

945.   Widmann, R. L. "An Iris Murdoch Checklist. "
        Critique: Studies in Modern Fiction 10 (1967):17-29.

946. Wiley, Paul L. "Iris Murdoch (1919-   )." In Paul
      L. Wiley, The British Novel: Conrad to the Present,
      pp. 88-90. Northbrook, Ill.: AHM Publishing Corp.,
      1973.

947. Wolfe, Peter. The Disciplined Heart: Iris Murdoch
      and her Novels. Columbia, Mo.: University of Mis-
      souri Press, 1966, pp. 216-20.

PART III

WRITINGS BY
MURIEL SPARK
(to 1975)

A. NOVELS

948.   The Abbess of Crewe: A Modern Morality Tale. London: Macmillan & Company, Ltd., 1st ed., 1974.
New York: Viking Press, 1974.

Reviews of The Abbess of Crewe

949.   Anonymous. Booklist 71 (15 October 1974):215,
240.

950.   _____. Books and Bookmen 20 (January
1975):28.

951.   _____. Choice 12 (March 1975):78.

952.   _____. Critic [Chicago] 33 (January-February 1975):75.

953.   _____. Kirkus Reviews 42 (15 August 1974):
900.

954.   _____. Observer [London], 10 November
1974, p. 33.

955.   _____. Time 104 (11 November 1974):112,
E5.

956.   _____. Virginia Quarterly Review 51 (Spring
1975):liv.

957.   Adams, Phoebe. Atlantic Monthly 234 (November 1974):123-24.

958.   Allen, Bruce. Library Journal 99 (1 November
1974):2873.

959.   Bannon, Barbara A. Publishers Weekly 206
(19 August 1974):74.

101

960.   Cooper, Susan. Christian Science Monitor, 13
        November 1974, p. 12.

961.   Crain, Jane Larkin. Saturday Review/World 2
        (19 October 1974):24, 28.

962.   Hill, William B. Best Sellers [University of
        Scranton, Pa.] 34 (15 November 1974):374.

963.   Malin, Irving. New Republic 171 (12 October
        1974):29-30.

964. The Bachelors. Harmondsworth, Middlesex, England:
      Penguin Books, Ltd., 1963.
      London: Macmillan & Company, Ltd., 1st ed., 1960.
      New York: St. Martin's Press, 1960.
      Philadelphia: J. B. Lippincott Company, 1961.
      Toronto: The Copp Clark Company, 1960.

             Translations of The Bachelors

965.   De Vrijgezellen. [No trans. given.] Amster-
        dam: Contact, 1962, 1963, and Amsterdam:
        Querido, 1966, 1969.

966.   Dokushinsha. Trans. by Akio Kudô. Tokyo:
        Shinchô-sha, 1962.

967.   Junggesellen. Trans. by Elizabeth Schnack.
        Zürich: Diogenes Verlag, 1961, and Reinbek,
        Germany: Rowohlt, 1968.

968.   Ungkarlarna. Trans. by Ingeborg von Rosen.
        Stockholm: Norstedt, 1962.

             Reviews of The Bachelors

969.   Anonymous. Booklist 57 (15 April 1961):520.

970.   _____ . British Book News no. 245 (Jan-
        uary 1961):76.

971.   _____ . Kirkus Reviews 29 (15 January
        1961):71.

972.   _____ . In Masterplots 1962 Annual, pp.
        27-30. Ed. by Frank N. Magill. New York:

Salem Press, 1962. Also in Masterplots Comprehensive Library Edition, vol. 1, pp. 318-20. Ed. by Frank N. Magill. New York: Salem Press, 1968 and in Survey of Contemporary Literature, vol. 1, pp. 291-94. Ed. by Frank N. Magill. New York: Salem Press, 1971.

973. _____. Times Weekly Review [London], 20 October 1960, p. 9.

974. Adams, Phoebe. Atlantic Monthly 207 (May 1961):104.

975. Evans, Fallon. Critic [Chicago] 19 (April-May 1961):28-29.

976. Fay, Elizabeth. Catholic Library World 32 (May-June 1961):533.

977. Hughes, Catharine. Catholic World 193 (August 1961):332-33.

978. Keown, Eric. Punch 239 (2 November 1960): 647.

979. McConkey, James. Epoch 11 (Spring 1961): 124-25.

980. Sheehan, E. America 104 (18 March 1961): 796.

981. Smith, William James. Commonweal 75 (8 December 1961):294.

982. Sullivan, Oona. Jubilee 8 (March 1961):47.

983. Wood, Frederick T. English Studies [Amsterdam] 42 (August 1961):260.

984. The Ballad of Peckham Rye. Harmondsworth, Middlesex, England: Penguin Books, Ltd., 1963. London: Macmillan & Company, Ltd., 1st ed., 1960. Philadelphia: J. B. Lippincott Company, 1960.

Translations of The Ballad of Peckham Rye

985. Balada Z Prédměstí. Trans. by Heda

Kovályová. Praha, Czechoslovakia: Odeon,
1970.

986.   Die Ballade von Peckham Rye. Trans. by
Elisabeth Schnack. Zürich: Diogenes Verlag,
1961.

987.   Balladen om Djävulens Sändebud. Trans. by
Ingeborg von Rosen. Stockholm: Norstedt,
1965.

988.   Balladan om Djaevelens Sendebud. Trans. by
Christopher Maaløe. Copenhagen: Spektrum,
1967.

Reviews of The Ballad of Peckham Rye

989.   Anonymous. Booklist 57 (1 October 1960):88.

990.   _____. British Book News no. 236 (April
1960):289.

991.   _____. Kirkus Reviews 28 (1 June 1960):430.

992.   _____. In Masterplots 1961 Annual, pp. 10-
13. Ed. by Frank N. Magill. New York:
Salem Press, 1961 and in Survey of Contemporary Literature, vol. 1, pp. 305-308. Ed. by
Frank N. Magill. New York: Salem Press,
1971.

993.   _____. New Yorker 36 (27 August 1960):
102.

994.   Furbank, P. N. Listener 65 (3 March 1960):
417.

995.   Hughes, Riley. Catholic World 192 (December
1960):182-83.

996.   Keown, Eric. Punch 238 (16 March 1960):399.

997.   Lanning, George. Kirkus Reviews [vol. un-
known] (Winter 1961):173.

998.   McConkey, James. Epoch 10 (Fall 1960):249-
51.

999. Mott, Schuyler L. Library Journal 85 (July 1960):2620.

1000. Pickrel, Paul. Harper's Magazine 221 (August 1960):99-100.

1001. Quinton, Anthony. London Magazine 7 (May 1960):78-81.

1002. West, Paul. New Statesman 59 (5 March 1960): 341.

1003. The Comforters. Harmondsworth, Middlesex, England: Penguin Books, Ltd., 1963.
London: Macmillan & Company, Ltd., 1st ed., 1957, 1958 and Skelton Robinson, 1957.
New York: Avon Books, 1965, paperback and The Macmillan Company, 1957.
Philadelphia: J. B. Lippincott Company, 1957, 1958.

Translations of The Comforters

1004. Los Consoladores. [No trans. given.] Santiago, Chile: Empresa Editorial Zig-Zag, 1968.

1005. Die Tröster. Trans. by Peter Naujack. Zürich: Diogenes Verlag, 1963; Frankfurt am Main and Berlin: Ullstein, 1968.

Reviews of The Comforters

1006. Anonymous. Booklist 54 (1 October 1957):77.

1007. _____. British Book News no. 200 (April 1957):254.

1008. _____. Saturday Review 48 (20 November 1965):40.

1009. The Driver's Seat. London: Macmillan & Company, Ltd., 1st ed., 1970.
New York: Alfred A. Knopf, Inc., 1970.

Translations of The Driver's Seat

1010. Forarsatet. Trans. by Erik Sandin. Stockholm: Norstedt, 1971.

1011. Førersaedet.   Trans. by Christopher Maaløe.
       Copenhagen: Gyldendal, 1971.

1012. Identikit.   Trans. by Masolino d'Amico.   Milan:
       Bompiani, 1971.

1013. Una Mujer al Volante.   Trans. by Andrés Bosch.
       Barcelona: Editorial Lumen, 1971.

       Reviews of The Driver's Seat

1014. Anonymous.   Antioch Review 30 (Fall-Winter
       1970-71):458-59.

1015. _____.   Books and Bookmen 20 (March
       1975):81.

1016. _____.   British Book News [no number] (De-
       cember 1970):984.

1017. _____.   Catholic Library World 42 (May
       1971):558.

1018. _____.   Choice 8 (September 1971):836.

1019. _____.   Observer [London], 12 May 1974,
       p. 33.

1020. _____.   Observer Colour Magazine [London],
       7 November 1971, pp. 73-74.

1021. Adams, Phoebe.   Atlantic Monthly 226 (October
       1970):150.

1022. Avant, John A.   Library Journal 95 (July 1970):
       2521.

1023. Davenport, Guy.   National Review 22 (17 No-
       vember 1970):1215-16.

1024. Frakes, J. R.   Chicago Tribune and Washing-
       ton Post Book World, 18 October 1970, p. 2.

1025. Easton, Elizabeth.   Saturday Review 53 (10
       October 1970):34, 65.

1026. Hill, William B.   America 123 (28 November
       1970):464.

1027. _____. Best Sellers 30 (1 November 1970):
      325.

1028. Kuehl, Linda. Commonweal 93 (15 January
      1971):378-79.

1029. Thomas, Edward. London Magazine n. s. 10
      (October 1970):95-98.

1030. Wade, Rosalind. Contemporary Review 218
      (January 1971):45-48.

1031. The Girls of Slender Means. Harmondsworth, Middle-
      sex, England: Penguin Books, Ltd., 1966.
      London: Macmillan & Company, Ltd., 1st ed., 1963.
      New York: Alfred A. Knopf, Inc., Avon Books, and
      St. Martin's Press, 1963.
      Toronto: The Copp Clark Company, 1963.

      Translations of The Girls of Slender Means

1032. Les Demoiselles de Petite Fortune. Trans. by
      Magdeleine Paz. Paris: R. Laffont, 1965.

1033. Fattiga Flickor. Trans. by Ingeborg von
      Rosen. Stockholm: Norstedt, 1964.

1034. Mädchen met Begrenzten Möglichkeiten. Trans.
      by Kyra Stromberg. Reinbek, Germany:
      Rowohlt, 1964, 1970.

1035. Meisjes met een Smalle Beurs. Trans. by
      Katja Vranken. Amsterdam and Antwerpen:
      Contact, 1966.

1036. Piger I Trange Kår. Trans. by Christopher
      Maaløe. Copenhagen: Spektrum, 1968.

1037. Le Ragazze di Pochi Mezzi. Trans. by Luisa
      Pantaleoni. Milan: Mondadori, 1966.

1038. Las Senoritas de Escasos Medios. Trans. by
      Andrés Bosch. Barcelona: Editorial Lumen,
      1967, 1968.

1039. Ubemidlede Piker Fra Gode Hjem. Trans. by
      Carl Frederick Prytz. Oslo: Gyldendal, 1964.

Reviews of <u>The Girls of Slender Means</u>

1040. Anonymous. <u>Booklist</u> 60 (15 October 1963):
       190.

1041. _____. <u>Observer Weekend Review</u> [London],
       31 July 1966, p. 18.

1042. _____. <u>Times Weekly Review</u> [London], 26
       September 1963, p. 11.

1043. _____. <u>Virginia Quarterly Review</u> 40 (Win-
       ter 1964):xiii.

1044. Brooke, Jocelyn. <u>Listener</u> 70 (26 September
       1963):481.

1045. Brophy, Brigid. <u>London Magazine</u> n. s. 3 (De-
       cember 1963):76-80.

1046. Gardiner, Harold C. <u>America</u> 109 (26 October
       1963):488.

1047. Grande, Brother Luke M. <u>Best Sellers</u> 23
       (15 October 1963):255.

1048. Hill, W. B. <u>America</u> 109 (23 November 1963):
       682.

1049. Hyman, Stanley E. <u>New Leader</u> 46 (16 Sep-
       tember 1963):17-18.

1050. Jackson, Katherine Gauss. <u>Harper's Magazine</u>
       227 (November 1963):137.

1051. Kelley, Mary E. <u>Library Journal</u> 88 (1 Oc-
       tober 1963):3647.

1052. Knowles, A. Sidney, Jr. In <u>Masterplots 1964
       Annual</u>, pp. 112-13. Ed. by Frank N. Magill.
       New York: Salem Press, 1964. Also in
       <u>Survey of Contemporary Literature</u>, vol. 3,
       pp. 1763-66. Ed. by Frank N. Magill. New
       York: Salem Press, 1971.

1053. Price, R. G. G. <u>Punch</u> 245 (25 September
       1963):470.

1054. W., G. Cosmopolitan 158 (September 1963):
25.

1055. Worthy, Judith. Books and Bookmen 11 (August 1966):64.

1056. The Hothouse by the East River. London: Macmillan & Company, Ltd., 1st ed., 1973.
New York: Viking Press, 1973.

Reviews of The Hothouse by the East River

1057. Anonymous. Choice 10 (September 1973):985.

1058. _____. Kirkus Reviews 41 (15 February 1973):212.

1059. _____. Virginia Quarterly Review 49 (Autumn 1973):cxxxvii.

1060. Adams, Phoebe. Atlantic Monthly 231 (May 1973):122.

1061. Bannon, Barbara A. Publishers Weekly 203 (5 March 1973):73.

1062. Bromwich, David. Commentary 56 (September 1973):85-90.

1063. Hill, William B. America 129 (17 November 1973):382.

1064. Howes, Victor. Christian Science Monitor, 30 May 1973, p. 9.

1065. Loprete, N. J. Best Sellers 33 (1 September 1973):246.

1066. Portis, Rowe. Library Journal 98 (1 March 1973):767-68.

1067. Price, Martin. Antioch Review 32 (November 1973):695.

1068. Prigozy, Ruth. Commonweal 99 (9 November 1973):136-38.

1069. The Mandelbaum Gate. Harmondsworth, Middlesex,

England: Penguin Books, Ltd., 1967.
London: Macmillan & Company, Ltd., 1st ed., 1965.
New York: Alfred A. Knopf, Inc., 1965.
Toronto: Macmillan & Company of Canada, Ltd.,
1965.

Translations of The Mandelbaum Gate

1070.   Mandelbaumin Portii.   Trans. by Juhani Jaska-
ri.   Porvoo and Helsinki, Finland: Werner
Söderström, 1966.

1071.   De Mandelbaumpoort.   Trans. by H. W. J.
Schaap.   Amsterdam: Contact, 1966, 1969.

1072.   Mandelbaum-Porten.   Trans. by Mogens Boisen.
Copenhagen: Spektrum, 1966.

1073.   Mandelbaumporten.   Trans. by Olov Jonason.
Stockholm: Norstedt, 1966, and Helsingfors:
H. Schildts, 1966.

1074.   Das Mandelbaumtor.   [No trans. given.]
Reinbek, Germany: Rowohlt, 1967.

1075.   La Porta di Mandelbaum.   Trans. by Ettore
Capriolo.   Milan: Mandadori, 1966; Milan:
Club Degli Editori, 1967; and Verona: Monda-
dori, 1967.

1076.   La Porte Mandelbaum.   Trans. by Pierre
Marly, Marie-Christine Mengin, and Robert
Mengin.   Paris: Buchet-Chastel, 1968.

Reviews of The Mandelbaum Gate

1077.   Anonymous.   Booklist 62 (15 October 1965):195.

1078.   _____ .   British Book News no. 306 (February 1966):163.

1079.   _____ .   Kirkus Reviews 33 (1 July 1965):646.

1080.   _____ .   Saturday Review 50 (29 April 1967):
32.

1081.   _____ .   Time 86 (5 November 1965):128.

1082. _____. Virginia Quarterly Review 42 (Summer 1966):xc.

1083. Betts, Doris. In Masterplots 1966 Annual, pp. 175-78. Ed. by Frank N. Magill. New York: Salem Press, 1965, 1967. Also in Survey of Contemporary Literature, vol. 4, pp. 2885-87. Ed. by Frank N. Magill. New York: Salem Press, 1971.

1084. Bresler, Riva T. Library Journal 90 (1 October 1965):4113.

1085. Brooke, Jocelyn. Listener 74 (14 October 1965):595.

1086. Cook, Roderick. Harper's Magazine 231 (November 1965):128-29.

1087. Fleischer, Leonore. Publishers Weekly 191 (20 February 1967):150.

1088. Grumbach, Doris. America 113 (23 October 1965):474-78.

1089. Johnson, Lucy. Progressive [Madison, Wis.] 29 (November 1965):41.

1090. McGuinness, Frank. London Magazine n. s. 5 (November 1965):94-98.

1091. Maloff, Saul. Commonweal 83 (3 December 1965):287.

1092. Petersen, Clarence. Chicago Tribune Books Today, 16 April 1967, p. 9.

1093. Shuttleworth, Martin. Punch 249 (20 October 1965):588.

1094. Wood, Frederick T. English Studies [Amsterdam] 47 (August 1966):315.

1095. Memento Mori. Harmondsworth, Middlesex, England: Penguin Books, Ltd., 1961.
London: Macmillan & Company, Ltd., 1st ed., 1959.
New York: Avon Books, Bard edition, 1971, 1974,

112   Muriel Spark

paperback; Meridian Books, 1960, paperback; and
Time, Inc., 1964.
Philadelphia: J. B. Lippincott Company, 1959.

Translations of Memento Mori

1096. Memento Mori. Trans. by J. B. Cuyás Boira.
Andorra la Vella: Editorial Andorra, 1968,
1969.

1097. Memento Mori. Trans. by Christopher Maaløe.
Copenhagen: Schønberg, 1960.

1098. Memento Mori. Trans. by Augusta Mattioli.
Milan and Verona: Mondadori, 1963.

1099. Memento Mori. Trans. by Peter Naujack.
Zürich: Diogenes Verlag, 1960; Frankfurt
am Main and Hamburg: Fischer Bücherei,
1963; and Stuttgart and Hamburg: Deutsch
Bücherbund, 1964.

1100. Memento Mori. Trans. by Magdeleine Paz.
Paris: Laffont, 1964.

1101. Memento Mori. Trans. by Ilona Róna. Budapest: Európa Kiadó, 1963.

1102. Memento Mori. Trans. by Krystyna Tarnowska.
Warsaw: Państw. Instytut Wydawn, 1970.

1103. Memento Mori. Trans. by Ingeborg von Rosen.
Stockholm: Norstedt, 1960.

1104. Memento Mori. Trans. by Katje Vranken.
Amsterdam: Contact, 1963, 1968.

Reviews of Memento Mori

1105. Anonymous. Best Sellers [University of Scran-
ton, Pa.] 31 (1 January 1972):452.

1106. _____. British Book News no. 225 (May
1959):354.

1107. _____. British Book News no. 249 (May
1961):381.

1108. _____. In Masterplots Comprehensive Library Edition, vol. 5, pp. 2991-93. Ed. by Frank N. Magill. New York: Salem Press, 1968.

1109. Bannon, Barbara A. Publishers Weekly 190 (24 October 1966):52.

1110. Elliott, Desmond. John O'London's Weekly 1 (December 1959):286.

1111. Lucas, Barbara. Twentieth Century 166 (September 1959):213-15.

1112. Petersen, Clarence. Chicago Tribune Books Today, 18 December 1966, p. 11.

1113. Quinton, Anthony. London Magazine 6 (September 1959):84-88.

1114. Not to Disturb. London: Macmillan & Company, Ltd., 1st ed., 1971.
New York: Viking Press, 1971, 1972.

Reviews of Not to Disturb

1115. Anonymous. Books and Bookmen 20 (March 1975):81.

1116. _____. Kirkus Reviews 40 (15 January 1972):95-96.

1117. _____. Observer [London], 28 April 1974, p. 33.

1118. Adams, Phoebe. Atlantic Monthly 229 (April 1972):128.

1119. Brown, F. J. Books and Bookmen 17 (January 1972):56-57.

1120. Cuffe, Edwin D. America 126 (29 April 1972): 467.

1121. Fielding, Gabriel. Critic [Chicago] 30 (July-August 1972):67-68.

114   Muriel Spark

1122. Frankel, Haskel. Saturday Review 55 (8 April
      1972):74.

1123. Hill, William B. America 126 (20 May 1972):
      549.

1124. _____. Best Sellers 32 (15 April 1972):42.

1125. Spacks, Patricia Meyer. Hudson Review 25
      (Autumn 1972):502-503.

1126. The Prime of Miss Jean Brodie. Harmondsworth,
      Middlesex, England: Penguin Books, Ltd., 1965.
      London: Macmillan & Company, Ltd., 1st ed., 1961.
      New York: Dell Publishing Co., Delta Books, 1964,
      1966, 1974, paperback and Simon & Schuster, 1966.
      In The World of Modern Fiction: European, Vol. 2,
      pp. 154-245. Ed. by Steven Marcus.
      Philadelphia: J. B. Lippincott Company, 1962, 1974.
      Toronto: The Copp Clark Company, 1961.
      [Muriel Spark's The Prime of Miss Jean Brodie was
      adapted for the stage first by John Wood and later by
      Jay Presson Allen. Wood's version was produced
      first in London at Wyndham's Theatre in 1966, Allen's
      first in Boston at Colonial Theatre, from December
      26, 1967 to January 6, 1968, then on Broadway at
      Helen Hayes Theatre in New York City, beginning
      January 9, 1968. On the basis of her stage acting
      version, Jay Presson Allen wrote a screenplay for the
      filming by 20th Century-Fox in 1968 of a motion pic-
      ture entitled "The Prime of Miss Jean Brodie," which
      was released in 1969.]

Translations of The Prime of Miss Jean Brodie

1127. Le Bel Age de Miss Brodie. Trans. by Mag-
      deleine Paz. Paris: Laffont, 1962.

1128. Gil Anni in Fiore Della Signorina Brodie.
      Trans. by Ida Omboni. Milan and Verona:
      Mondadori, 1964.

1129. Juffrouw Brodies Beste Jaren. Trans. by
      W. A. C. Whitlau. Amsterdam and Antwerpen:
      Contact, 1965.

1130. Die Lehrerin. Trans. by Peter Naujack.

Zürich: Diogenes Verlag, 1962, and Reinbek, Germany: Rowohlt, 1969.

1131. Miss Jean Brodies Bästa År. Trans. by Ingeborg von Rosen. Stockholm: Norstedt, 1963, and Stockholm: Vingförl, 1964.

1132. La Primavera de Una Solterona. Trans. by Augusto Gubler. Santiago, Chile: Empresa Editorial Zig-Zag, 1969.

1133. El Punt Dolç de la Senyoreta Brodie. Trans. by Manuel de Pedrolo. Barcelona: Edicions 62, 1967.

Reviews of The Prime of Miss Jean Brodie

1134. Anonymous. Booklist 58 (1 February 1962): 342.

1135. _____. British Book News no. 256 (December 1961):877.

1136. _____. In Masterplots 1963 Annual, pp. 199-201. Ed. by Frank N. Magill. New York: Salem Press, 1963. Also in Survey of Contemporary Literature, vol. 5, pp. 3689-91. Ed. by Frank N. Magill. New York: Salem Press, 1971.

1137. _____. Time 79 (19 January 1962):89.

1138. _____. Times Weekly Review [London], 9 November 1961, p. 12.

1139. _____. Virginia Quarterly Review 38 (Autumn 1962):cv-cvi.

1140. Adams, Phoebe. Atlantic Monthly 209 (February 1962):122.

1141. Boegel, Joan P. Library Journal 87 (1 January 1962):114.

1142. Bradbury, Malcolm. Punch 241 (8 November 1961):696.

1143. Diamond, Naomi. Books Abroad 36 (Summer
       1962):323-24.

1144. Doyle, Edward. Book-of-the-Month Club News
       [New York], March 1962, p. 9.

1145. Fitzgibbon, William C. New York Times, 17
       January 1962, p. 31.

1146. Gardiner, Harold C. America 106 (27 Jan-
       uary 1962):564.

1147. Hope, Francis. Encounter 17 (December 1961):
       75, 78.

1148. Hughes, Catherine. Catholic World 194 (March
       1962):374-76.

1149. Page, William Lloyd. Smith's Trade News
       [London], 7 October 1961, p. 48.

1150. Petersen, Clarence. Chicago Tribune Books
       Today, 27 February 1966, p. 13.

1151. Wood, Frederick T. English Studies [Amster-
       dam] 43 (June 1962):209-10.

1152. The Public Image. Harmondsworth, Middlesex, Eng-
       land: Penguin Books, Ltd., 1970.
       London and Melbourne: Macmillan & Company, Ltd.,
       1st ed., 1968.
       New York: Alfred A. Knopf, Inc., 1968.

       Translations of The Public Image

1153. Ansiktet Utåt. Trans. by Ingeborg von Rosen.
       Stockholm: Norstedt, 1969.

1154. L'Image Publique. Trans. by Marie-Christine
       Mengin and Robert Mengin. Paris: Buchet-
       Chastel, 1969.

1155. De Image van een Filmster. Trans. by H. W. J.
       Schaap. Amsterdam: Contact, 1969.

1156. La Imagen Pública. Trans. by Andrés Bosch.
       Barcelona: Editorial Lumen, 1970.

1157. In den Augen der Öffentlichkeit. Trans. by
Christian Ferber. Reinbek, Germany:
Rowohlt, 1969.

1158. A Közönség Bálványa. Trans. by István Bart.
Budapest: Európa Kiadó, 1971.

1159. Lice Za Publikata. Trans. by Zivoko Kefalov.
Sofia, Bulgaria: Nar. Kultura, 1971.

1160. I Publikum Øjne. Trans. by Christopher
Maaløe. Copenhagen: Gyldendal, 1969.

Reviews of The Public Image

1161. Anonymous. Booklist 65 (15 November 1968):
353.

1162. _____. Kirkus Reviews 36 (15 July 1968):
780.

1163. Bannon, Barbara A. Publishers Weekly 194
(5 August 1968):53.

1164. Boyce, Daniel F. In Masterplots 1969 Annual, pp. 268-71. Ed. by Frank N. Magill.
New York: Salem Press, 1970. Also in Survey of Contemporary Literature, vol. 6, pp.
3739-42. Ed. by Frank N. Magill. New
York: Salem Press, 1971.

1165. Grumbach, Doris. America 119 (26 October
1968):387-88.

1166. Hill, William B. Best Sellers 28 (1 November 1968):319.

1167. Hoagland, Joan M. Library Journal 93 (August 1968):2899.

1168. Jackson, Katherine Gauss. Harper's Magazine
237 (November 1968):159-60.

1169. Price, R. G. G. Punch 254 (12 June 1968):
864.

1170. Pryce-Jones, David. London Magazine n. s.

8 (July 1968):106, 108.

1171. Robinson. Harmondsworth, Middlesex, England: Penguin Books, Ltd., 1964.
London: Macmillan & Company, Ltd., 1st ed., 1958.
New York: Avon Books, 1969, 1974, paperback.
Philadelphia: J. B. Lippincott Company, 1958, 1963.

Translations of Robinson

1172. Robinson. Trans. by Cármen Cienfuegos.
Santiago, Chile: Empresa Editorial Zig-Zag, 1969.

1173. Robinson. Trans. by Elizabeth Gilbert.
Zürich: Diogenes Verlag, 1962, Frankfurt
am Main: Ullstein, 1967, and Frankfurt am
Main and Berlin: Rowohlt, 1970.

Reviews of Robinson

1174. Anonymous. British Book News no. 217 (September 1958):634.

1175. Hughes, Riley. Catholic World 189 (May 1959): 162-63.

1176. Quigly, Isabel. Encounter 60 (September 1958): 82-84.

1177. Richardson, Maurice. New Statesman 56 (5 July 1958):25.

B. CRITICAL ESSAYS

1178. [Title unknown.] Daily Express [London], 25 April 1963, p. 17. [Spark comments: "Too many people suffer from boredom and loneliness.... I've known considerable loneliness. It's something I've written about and regard as a major problem in our society."]

1179. [Title unknown.] Daily Telegraph [London], 25 September 1970, p. 15. [Spark explains her move from New York to Rome: "New York was beginning to decay," and "it was getting dangerous and dirty."]

1180. "Author and Critic." Times Literary Supplement [London], 4 October 1963, p. 787. [Letter to the Editor concerning the publication of Derek Stanford's Muriel Spark.]

1181. "The Brontës as Teachers." New Yorker 41 (22 January 1966):30-33.

1182. "The Desegregation of Art." Proceedings of the American Academy of Arts and Letters and the National Institute of Arts and Letters, second series, no. 21 (1971):21-27. [Annual Blashfield Foundation Address]

1183. "Exotic Departures." New Yorker 42 (28 January 1967):31-32.

1184. "Introduction." Forum Stories and Poems [London] 1, no. 1 (Summer 1949):1.

1185. "Mary Shelley: A Prophetic Novelist." Listener 49 (22 February 1951):305-306.

1186. "The Mystery of Job's Suffering." Church of England Newspaper, 15 April 1955, p. 7.

1187. "The Poet in Mr. Eliot's Ideal State." Outposts

[Manchester, England] no. 14 (Summer 1949):26-28.

1188. "Poetry or Exam Paper." Poetry Quarterly [London]
12 (Spring 1950):62. [Letter to the Editor]

1189. "The Religion of an Agnostic--A Sacramental View of
the World in the Writings of Proust." Church of England Newspaper, 27 November 1953, p. 1.

1190. "St. Monica." In Saints and Ourselves, third series,
pp. 26-37. Ed. by Philip Camaran, S. J. London:
Hollis & Carter, and New York: P. J. Kenedy &
Sons, 1958.

1191. "Speaking of Writing--I." Times [London], 21 November 1963, p. 18. [The Girls of Slender Means]

1192. "Taxing Ideas." Tablet [London] 206 (17 December
1955):599-600.

1193. Spark, Muriel, and Stanford, Derek. "Introduction."
Forum Stories and Poems [London] 1, no. 2 (1949):
25-26.

C.   AUTOBIOGRAPHICAL ESSAYS

1194.   [A conversation with Philip Toynbee.] In Muriel
Spark Limited Edition, overpage. [No editor given.]
London: Observer Art, 1971.

1195.   "Edinburgh-born." New Statesman 64 (10 August 1962):
180.

1196.   "How I Became a Novelist." Broadcast in the B. B. C.
Programme, "Two of a Kind" on 26 April 1960. Tran-
script of the B. B. C. Programme "Two of a Kind" is
published in Books and Bookmen 7 (November 1961):9,
and in John O'London's 3 (1 December 1960):683.
[Spark discusses "The Seraph and the Zambesi," The
Comforters, Robinson, Memento Mori, The Ballad of
Peckham Rye, and The Bachelors.]

1197.   "My Conversion." Twentieth Century 170 (Autumn
1961):58-63.

1198.   "The Poet's House." Critic [Chicago] 19 (February-
March 1961):15-16. Also in Encounter 30 (May 1968):
48-50.

1199.   Transcript of a Granada television interview with Mal-
colm Muggeridge. [Title unknown.] [Cited by Peter
Kemp in his Muriel Spark. London: Paul Elek Books
Ltd., 1974, pp. 10, 27, 97, 130.]

1200.   "What Images Return." In Memoirs of a Modern Scotland, pp. 151-53. Ed. by Karl Miller. London:
Faber & Faber, Ltd., 1970.

D. PLAYS

1201. Spark, Muriel, and Holme, Christopher. "The Ballad of Peckham Rye. " [A stage version of Spark's novel by the same title. In two acts, prose and verse. First performance, August 17, 1965, at Salzburg, Landestheater (Europa Studio).]

Review of "The Ballad of Peckham Rye"

1202. Kienzle, Siegfried. Modern World Theatre: A Guide to Productions in Europe and the United States Since 1945. Trans. from the German by Alexander Henderson and Elizabeth Henderson. New York: Frederick Ungar Publishing Co., 1970, pp. 418-19.

1203. "Doctors of Philosophy. " In Novelists' Theatre, pp. 101-279. Introduction by Eric Rhode. Harmondsworth, Middlesex, England, and Ringwood, Victoria, Australia: Penguin Books, Ltd., 1966.
London: Macmillan & Company, Ltd., 1st ed., 1963, 1966.
New York: Alfred A. Knopf, Inc., 1966.
[A play in three acts, prose. First performance October 2, 1962, London, New Arts Theatre Club. Presented by Michael Codon, directed by Donald McWinnie, designed by Hutchinson Scott.]

Reviews of "Doctors of Philosophy"

1204. Anonymous. Booklist 62 (15 March 1966):691-92.

1205. _____ . British Book News no. 277 (September 1963):683.

1206. _____ . Choice 4 (September 1967):698.

1207.   . In New York Times Theater Re-
       views 1920-1970. Vol. 7/1960-1966. New
       York: The New York Times and Arno Press,
       1971. [Page is designated as 4 October 1962.]
       [Review of performance at the New Arts Theatre
       in London on 2 October 1962.]

1208.   . Times Literary Supplement [London],
       19 July 1963, p. 530.

1209. Adams, Phoebe. Atlantic Monthly 217 (April
       1966):152.

1210. Kienzle, Siegfried. Modern World Theatre:
       A Guide to Productions in Europe and the United
       States Since 1945. Trans. from the German
       by Alexander Henderson and Elizabeth Hender-
       son. New York: Frederick Ungar Publishing
       Co., 1970, pp. 418-19.

1211. Lerner, Arthur. Books Abroad 40 (Autumn
       1966):465.

1212. Pepper, G. M. National Review 18 (5 April
       1966):327.

1213. "The Dry River Bed." Critic [Chicago] 20 (October-
       November 1961):31-37. [A radio play.]

1214. "The Interview." Transatlantic Review [London] no.
       4 (Summer 1960):69-88. [A one-act play for radio.]

1215. Allen, Jay Presson. "The Prime of Miss Jean Bro-
       die." New York, Hollywood, London, and Toronto:
       Samuel French, Inc., 1969. [A stage version of the
       novel, The Prime of Miss Jean Brodie, by Muriel
       Spark. First performance was in Boston at Colonial
       Theatre, December 26, 1967 to January 6, 1968, then
       on Broadway at Helen Hayes Theatre in New York,
       running 379 performances, beginning January 9, 1968.]

Reviews of "The Prime of Miss Jean Brodie"

1216. Barnes, Clive. New York Times, 25 January
       1968, p. 32. Also in New York Times Theater
       Reviews 1920-1970. V. 8/1967-1970, 26 Janu-
       ary 1968 [pages are not numbered].

1217. _____ . New York Times, 28 January 1968,
p. 11. Also in New York Times Theater Reviews 1920-1970. V. 8/1967-1970, 27 January
1968 [pages are not numbered].

1218. _____ . In New York Times Theater Reviews
1920-1970. V. 8/1967-1970. New York: The
New York Times and Arno Press, 1971 [pages
are designated as January 17, 26, 27, 1968].
[Reviews of "The Prime of Miss Jean Brodie"
performance at the Helen Hayes Theatre in
New York, January 1968.]

1219. Gottfried, Martin. New York Theatre Critics'
Reviews 29 [week of 22 January 1968]:383.

E. POEMS

1220. "Anniversary. " Variegation [Los Angeles] 3 (Autumn 1948):17.

1221. "Autumn. " Poetry Review [London] 38 (March-April 1947):155-56.

1222. "The Beads. " Poetry Quarterly [London] 11 (Autumn 1949):144-45.

1223. "The Bells at Bray. " Poetry Review [London] 38 (September-October 1947):353.

1224. "Birthday. " Poetry Review [London] 38 (July-August 1947):270.

1225. "Birthday Acrostic. " Poetry Quarterly [London] 13 (Summer 1951):68.

1226. "Bluebell among the Sables. " In Springtime Two, pp. 73-74. Ed. by Peter Owen and Wendy Owen. London: Peter Owen Ltd. , 1958. Also in Transatlantic Review no. 10 (Summer 1962):48-49.

1227. "Cadmus. " Poetry Review [London] 38 (September-October 1947):379.

1228. "Canaan. " New Yorker 42 (16 April 1966):48.

1229. "The Card Party. " New Yorker 39 (28 December 1963):30.

1230. "Chrysalis. " Ladies Home Journal 83 (February 1966): 122.

1231. "Conundrum. " Chanticleer [London] 1 (Autumn 1952): 14.

1232. "The Dancers." World Review n. s. 12 (February 1950):30.

1233. "Day of Rest." Recurrence: A Quarterly of Rhyme [Los Angeles] 3 (Autumn 1952):56.

1234. "Edinburgh Villanelle." New Yorker 43 (26 August 1967):24.

1235. "Elegy in a Kensington Churchyard." Fortnightly n. s. 168 (September 1950):191.

1236. "Elementary." World Review n. s. 29 (July 1951):21. Also in Springtime Two, p. 74. Ed. by Peter Owen and Wendy Owen. London: Peter Owen Ltd., 1958.

1237. "Faith and Works." Aylesford Review: A Carmelite Quarterly [Wales] 2 (Winter 1957-58):37.

1238. "Four People in a Neglected Garden." Poetry Quarterly [London] 13 (Autumn 1951):122-23.

1239. "Frantic a Child Ran." Poetry of Today: New Verse Supplement to Poetry Review (1946):80.

1240. "Fruitless Fable." Reporter 37 (7 September 1967):44.

1241. "The Grave that Time Dug." World Review n. s. 32 (October 1951):68.

1242. "Holy Water Rondel." Catholic World 184 (November 1956):134. Also in Springtime Three, pp. 102-103. Ed. by Peter Owen and Michael Levien. London: Peter Owen Ltd., 1961.

1243. "Indian Feathers." Variegation [Los Angeles] 4 (Autumn 1949):4.

1244. "Invocation to a Child." Poetry Quarterly [London] 10 (Spring 1948):22.

1245. "Leaning over an Old Wall." Poetry Review [London] 38 (March-April 1947):106.

1246. "A Letter at Christmas." Outposts [Manchester, England] no. 20 (1952):5-6.

1247. "A Letter to Howard." Poetry Quarterly [London] 10 (Autumn 1948):152-53.

1248. "Liturgy of Time Past." Atlantic Monthly 216 (August 1965):91.

1249. "Lost Lover." Outposts [Manchester, England] no. 11 (Autumn 1948):3.

1250. "Magdalen." Gemini: A Pamphlet Magazine of New Poetry [Derby, England] no. 1 (May 1949): [pages unknown].

1251. "Messengers." New Yorker 43 (16 September 1967): 44.

1252. "The Nativity." Poetry Quarterly [London] 13 (Winter 1951-52):158-62.

1253. "No Need for Shouting." Poetry Quarterly [London] 13 (Spring 1951):24.

1254. "Note by the Wayside." Atlantic Monthly 216 (November 1965):102.

1255. "Omega." Poetry Review [London] 38 (November-December 1947):519.

1256. "Omen." Outposts [Manchester, England] no. 15 (Winter 1949):16.

1257. "On the Lack of Sleep." New Yorker 39 (7 December 1963):58.

1258. "Pearl Miners." Poetry [Chicago] 82 (September 1953):318-20.

1259. "Poem." Prospect [Little Chalfont, England] 11 (Summer 1948):26.

1260. "Portrait." Recurrence: A Quarterly of Rhyme [Los Angeles] 2 (Autumn 1951):7.

1261. "The Robe and the Song." Poetry Review [London] 38 (May-June 1947):192-93. Also in Poems I Remember, [pages unknown]. Ed. by Christmas Humphries. London: Michael Joseph, 1960.

1262.   "She Wolf." New Yorker 42 (4 February 1967):40.

1263.   "She Wore his Luck on her Breast." Outposts [Manchester, England] no. 12 (Winter 1948):10.

1264.   "Shipton-Under-Wychwood." Public Opinion [London] 178 (11 August 1950):15.

1265.   "Sin." Punch 215 (27 October 1948):395.

1266.   "Song." Outposts [Manchester, England] no. 9 (Winter 1947):10.

1267.   "Song of the Divided Lover." Poetry Commonwealth [London] no. 1 (Summer 1948):5.

1268.   "Spring Hat 1946." Poetry Review [London] 37 (August-September 1946):328.

1269.   "Standing in Dusk." Variegation [Los Angeles] 3 (Summer 1948):5.

1270.   "This Plato." Arena [New Zealand] no. 21 (June 1949):12-13.

1271.   "Three Thoughts in Africa (October, 1943)." Poetry of Today: New Verse Supplement to Poetry Review [no vol.] (1946):81-82.

1272.   "Tracing the Landscape...." Poetry Commonwealth [London] no. 2. (Autumn 1948):5.

1273.   "Variations on Intuition." Variegation [Los Angeles] 4 (Spring 1949):16.

1274.   "The Victoria Falls." Poetry Review [London] 37 (August-September 1946):285.

1275.   "The Voice of One Lost Sings its Gain." Poetry Quarterly [London] 11 (Winter 1949):221.

1276.   "We Were Not Expecting the Prince Today." Recurrence: A Quarterly of Rhyme [Los Angeles] 1 (Winter 1951):15.

1277.   "The Well." Poetry Review [London] 38 (January-February 1947):82-86. [A prize-winning poem]

1278. "You, Dreamer." <u>Canadian Poetry Magazine</u> 2
      (March 1948):23.

1279. Spark, Muriel, and Stanford, Derek. "The Miners."
      <u>Chanticleer</u> [London] 1 (Autumn 1952):10.

F. SHORT STORIES

1280. "Alice Long's Dachshunds." New Yorker 43 (1 April 1967):36-40.

1281. "Bang-Bang You're Dead." In Winter's Tales 4, pp. 205-48. [No editor given.] London: Macmillan & Company, Ltd. and New York: St. Martin's Press, 1958.

1282. "The Curtain Blown by the Breeze." London Magazine 8 (January 1961):14-25.

1283. "Daisy Overend." World Review n. s. 42 (August 1952):48-52.

1284. "The Dark Glasses." In Winter's Tales 6, pp. 220-40 [1960 Macmillan edition]. Ed. by A. D. Maclean. London: Macmillan & Company, Ltd., 1960; New York: St. Martin's Press, 1960; and Nendeln, Liechtenstein, Switzerland: Kraus Reprint, 1969.

1285. "The Driver's Seat." New Yorker 46 (16 May 1970): 38-48, 50, 52, 55-56, 58, 61-62, 64, 66, 69-70, 72-74, 76, 84, 86-88, 91-94, 96, 99-102. [Also published as a novel.]

1286. "The End of Summer Time." London Mystery Magazine 37 (June 1958):65-69.

1287. "A garota que ficow a minha espera." In Misterio Magazine de Ellery Queen [Brazil] no. 101 (December 1957): [pages unknown].

1288. "The Gentile Jewess." New Yorker 39 (22 June 1963): 30. Also in Winter's Tales 9, pp. 235-46. Ed. by A. D. Maclean. London: Macmillan & Company, Ltd., and New York: St. Martin's Press, 1963. [First published in New Yorker 39 (22 June 1963):30.]

1289.   "The Girl I Left Behind Me. " Norseman 16 (January-
        February 1958):63-65.

1290.   "The Girls of Slender Means. " [A condensed version
        of the novel The Girls of Slender Means.] Saturday
        Evening Post 236 (14 December 1963):50-58, 60-63.

1291.   "Harper and Wilton. " In Pick of Today's Short Sto-
        ries, no. 4, pp. 191-94. Ed. by John Pudney. Lon-
        don: Putnam & Co. , Ltd. , 1953.

1292.   "The House of the Famous Poet. " Norseman 10 (No-
        vember-December 1952):420-26. Also in New Yorker
        42 (2 April 1966):46-50, and in Winter's Tales 12,
        pp. 160-70. Ed. by A. D. Maclean. London, Mel-
        bourne, and Toronto: Macmillan & Company, Ltd. ,
        and New York: St. Martin's Press, 1966.

1293.   "La Jovan Que abandone. " Coleccion De Misterio El-
        lery Queen [Mexico] vol. 23 [no date]: [pages un-
        known].

1294.   "Ladies and Gentlemen. " Chance: New Writing and
        Art 3rd issue (April-June 1953):40-46. Also in
        Transatlantic Review no. 9 (Spring 1962):107-14.

1295.   "The Leaf Sweeper. " London Mystery Magazine 31
        (December 1956):7-11. Also in A Partridge in a Pear
        Tree, pp. 70-75. Arranged by Neville Braybrooke.
        London: Darton, Longman & Todd; and Westminister,
        Md. : Newman Press, 1960.

1296.   "The Mandelbaum Gate. " New Yorker 41 (15 May
        1965):54-59, (10 July 1965):25-32, (24 July 1965):26-
        34, and (7 August 1965):28-34. [This story appeared
        in four installments as indicated.]

1297.   "A Member of the Family. " Mademoiselle 52 (Feb-
        ruary 1961):88, 136-39.

1298.   "Miss Pinkerton's Apocalypse. " Courier [London] 25
        (July 1955):81-83.

1299.   "The Ormolu Clock. " New Yorker 36 (17 September
        1960):38-41.

1300.   "The Pawnbroker's Wife. " Norseman 11 (July-August
        1953):271-79.

1301. "The Pearly Shadow. " Norseman 13 (November-De-
       cember 1955):421-22.

1302. "The Portobello Road. " Botteghe Oscure [Rome] 18
       (1956):98-122.   Also in Winter's Tales 2, pp. 272-
       308.   [No editor given.] London: Macmillan & Com-
       pany, Ltd. , and New York: St. Martin's Press,
       1956; also in Spine Chillers [pages unknown].   Ed. by
       Elizabeth Lee. London: Elek, 1961. [First published
       in Botteghe Oscure [Rome] 18 (1956):98-122.]

1303. "The Prime of Miss Jean Brodie. " New Yorker 37
       (14 October 1961):52-62, 64, 67, 68-69, 72-74, 77-78,
       80-82, 84, 87-88, 90-92, 94, 97-100, 102, 107-108,
       110-11, 114, 116-18, 123-24, 126-28, 131, 132, 134,
       136-38, 141-48, 151-58, 161. [Also published in
       1961 by Macmillan & Company, Ltd. of London, and
       later by others as a novel with the same title.]

1304. "The Quest for Lavishes Ghast. " Esquire 62 (Decem-
       ber 1964):216, 218.   Also in Winter's Tales 11, pp.
       202-206.   Ed. by A. D. Maclean.   London, Melbourne,
       and Toronto: Macmillan & Company, Ltd. , and New
       York: St. Martin's Press, 1965.

1305. "The Seraph and the Zambesi. " [The Observer Prize-
       Winning Christmas Story.] Observer [London] 23
       (December 1951):2.   Also in The Observer Prize Sto-
       ries [London], pp. 1-12.   Introduction by Elizabeth
       Bowen. London, Melbourne, and Toronto: William
       Heinemann, Ltd. , 1952.

1306. The Seraph and the Zambesi.   Philadelphia: J. B.
       Lippincott Company, 1960. [A privately printed, gift
       edition.]

1307. "The Twins. " Norseman 12 (March-April 1954):119-
       25.

1308. "You Should Have Seen the Mess. " Punch 234 (28
       May 1958):704-706.

G. CHILDREN'S BOOKS

1309. The French Window. London: Macmillan & Company, Ltd., 1970.

1310. The Very Fine Clock. Drawings by Edward Gorey. London: Macmillan & Company, Ltd., 1969. New York: Alfred A. Knopf, Inc., 1st ed., 1968.

Translation of The Very Fine Clock

1311. Spark, Muriel, and Gorey, Edward. Die Sehr Gute Uhr. Trans. by Gerd Haffmans. Zürich: Diogenes Verlag, 1971.

Reviews of The Very Fine Clock

1312. Harmon, Elva. Library Journal 94 (15 June 1969):2497-98.

1313. Maddocks, Melvin. Christian Science Monitor, 7 November 1968, p. B4.

1314. Pippett, Aileen. New York Times Book Review, 29 December 1968, p. 20.

1315. Russ, Lavinia. Publishers' Weekly 194 (11 November 1968):50.

H. LITERARY CRITICISM

1316. Child of Light: A Reassessment of Mary Wollstone-
craft Shelley. Folcroft, Pa.: Folcroft Library Editions, 1974.
Hadleigh, Essex, England: Tower Bridge Publications, Ltd., 1st ed., 1951.
New York: Avon Books, 1974.
Philadelphia: Richard West, 1974, hardbound reprint
of 1951 edition.
Port Washington, N. Y.: Kennikat Press, 1974.

Review of Child of Light

    1317. Koszul, A. Etudes Anglaises [Paris] 5 (August
    1952):256-58.

1318. "The Dramatic Works of T. S. Eliot." Women's Review no. 5 (1949): [pages unknown].

1319. Spark, Muriel, and Stanford, Derek. Emily Brontë:
Her Life and Work [Part One: Biographical, by
Spark; Part Two: Critical, by Stanford]. Hollywood-
by-the-Sea, Fla.: Transatlantic Arts, Inc., 1963.
London, New York, and Westfalen, Germany: British
Book Centre, Inc., 1953.
London: Macmillan & Company, Ltd., new ed.,
1966; and Peter Owen, Ltd., 1st ed., 1953, 1960,
1966.
New York: Coward-McCann, Inc., 1966.
New York and London: House & Maxwell, 1960.
Toronto: The Copp Clark Company, 1953.

Reviews of Emily Brontë: Her Life and Work

    1320. Anonymous. British Book News no. 161 (Jan-
    uary 1954):53.

    1321. _____ . British Book News no. 314 (October

134

1966):788.

1322. _____. English Journal [Champaign, Ill.]
49 (October 1960):509.

1323. _____. Kirkus Reviews 34 (1 September
1966):929.

1324. _____. Library Journal 91 (15 October
1966):5271-72.

1325. _____. Listener 51 (14 January 1954):109.

1326. _____. New Statesman and Nation 46 (19
December 1953):804.

1327. Blondell, J. Etudes Anglaises [Paris] 8 (July-
September 1955):269-70.

1328. Burke, Herbert. Library Journal 85 (August
1960):2792.

1329. Cook, Roderick. Harper's Magazine 233
(September 1966):114-15.

1330. Wilson, Elizabeth. English [Oxford, England]
10 (Spring 1955):147-48.

1331. John Masefield. London: Macmillan & Company, Ltd.,
1962; and Peter Nevill, Ltd., 1st ed., 1953.
Philadelphia: Richard West, 1973, hardbound reprint
of 1953 edition.
Toronto: The Copp Clark Company, 1962.

Reviews of John Masefield

1332. Anonymous. British Book News no. 158 (October 1953):155-56.

1333. _____. Listener 50 (3 September 1953):398.

1334. _____. Scottish Secondary Teachers Association Magazine [Glasgow] 8 (February 1954):
58.

1335. Farmer, A. J. Etudes Anglaises [Paris] 8
(July-September 1955):270.

1336. K., H. T. <u>Canadian Forum</u> 34 (April 1954):
       21-22.

1337. "Views and Reviews: The Poetry of Anne Brontë."
       <u>New English Weekly,</u> 26 May 1949, pp. 78-80. Also
       in <u>Women's Review</u> no. 6 (1949): [pages unknown].

1338. Spark, Muriel, et al. "Writers in the Tense Present."
       [An interview by Elizabeth Jane Howard.] <u>Queen:</u>
       <u>The Lady's Newspaper and Court Chronicle</u> [London]
       Centenary Issue (August 1961):135-46.

I. BOOK REVIEWS

1339. Review of The Apple and the Spectroscope, by Thomas R. Henn. Poetry Quarterly [London] 13 (Autumn 1951):139-44.

1340. Review of Beyond the Terminus of Stars, by Hugo Manning. Poetry Quarterly [London] 11 (Summer 1949):122-23.

1341. Review of Catullus, trans. by Jack Lindsay. Outposts [Manchester, England] no. 15 (Winter 1949):30-31.

1342. Review of Edith Sitwell, by C. M. Bowra, and The Drowned Sailor, by James Kirkup. Outposts [Manchester, England] no. 12 (Winter 1948):19-20.

1343. Review of In Wake of Wind, by Gloria Komai. Fortnightly 167 (February 1950):132-33.

1344. Review of The Lady with the Unicorn, by Vernon Watkins. Outposts [Manchester, England] no. 13 (Spring 1949):32-33.

1345. Review of The Modern Everyman, by Michael Burn. World Review [no vol.] (January 1949):78.

1346. Review of Poetry Awards, ed. by Robert T. Moore. Poetry Commonwealth [London] no. 7 (Summer 1950): 19-20.

1347. "Cecil Day Lewis." Poetry Quarterly [London] 11 (Autumn 1949):162-68. [Review of Poems 1943-1947, by Cecil Day Lewis.]

1348. "The Complete Frost." Public Opinion [London] 179 (30 March 1951):21-22. [Review of The Complete Poems of Robert Frost (no editor).]

1349. "Minor Victorian." Observer Weekend Review [Lon-

don], 19 February 1961, p. 29. [Review of Father
Faber, by Ronald Chapman.]

1350.   "Passionate Humbug." Public Opinion [London] 179
(23 February 1951):20. [Review of Queens of the
Circulating Library, ed. by Allan Walbank.]

1351.   "A Post Romantic." Poetry Quarterly [London] 14
(Summer 1952):59-60. [Review of The Poems of
Arthur Hugh Clough, ed. by H. F. Lowry, et al.]

1352.   "The Stricken Deer." Poetry Quarterly [London] 13
(Summer 1951):89-90. [Review of William Cowper,
by Norman Nicholson.]

1353.   "Three Vintages." Poetry Quarterly [London] 11
(Winter 1949):252-56. [Review of The Canticle of the
Rose, by Edith Sitwell; Collected Poems, by Louis
MacNeice; and The Pythoness, by Kathleen Raine.]

1354.   "Top Cats on Show." Observer [London], Christmas
Books Section, 29 November 1951, p. 4. [Review of
six books: Cats in Colour, by Stevie Smith; Cat's
Cradle, by Paul Dehn; A Book of Cats, by Dorothy
Margaret Stuart; All These and Kittens, Too, by
Frank Crew; Top Off the Milk, by Warren Chetham-
Strode; and Cats in May, by Doreen Tovey.]

1355.   "What You Say, and How You Say It." Poetry Quar-
terly [London] 12 (Winter 1950-51):234-37. [Review
of Andrew Young--Collected Poems, by Joan Hassall;
The Season's Pause, by W. J. Strachan; Underworlds,
by Frances Scarfe; Mountains Beneath the Horizon, by
William Bell; The Voice of Poetry, ed. by Hermann
Peschmann; and The Pleasures of Poetry, by Anthony
Bertram.]

J.   EDITORIALS

1356.   "The Catholic View." Poetry Review [London] 38
(November-December 1947):402-405.

1357.   "Criticism, Effect and Morals." Poetry Review
[London] 39 (January-February 1948):3-6.

1358. "A Pamphlet from the U. S. A. " Poetry Review [London] 39 (October-November 1948):318.

1359. "Poetry and the Other Arts. " Poetry Review [London] 39 (December 1948-January 1949):390.

1360. "Reassessment. " Poetry Review [London] 39 (April-May 1948):103-104.

1361. "Reassessment--II. " Poetry Review [London] 39 (August-September 1948):234-36.

K. COLLECTED WORKS

1362. Collected Poems I. London and Melbourne: Mac-
millan & Company, Ltd., 1st ed., 1967.
New York: Alfred A. Knopf, Inc., 1968.
Toronto: Macmillan Company of Canada, Ltd., 1967.

Reviews of Collected Poems I

1363. Anonymous. Booklist 65 (1 November 1968):
285.

1364. _____. British Book News no. 332 (April
1968):294-95.

1365. _____. Kirkus Reviews 36 (15 April 1968):
504.

1366. Cushman, Jerome. Library Journal 93 (1
June 1968):2246.

1367. Kitching, Jessie B. Publishers' Weekly 193
(22 April 1968):48.

1368. Press, John. Punch 254 (7 February 1968):
211.

1369. Taylor, Henry. In Masterplots 1969 Annual,
pp. 69-72. Ed. by Frank N. Magill. New
York: Salem Press, 1969. Also in Survey of
Contemporary Literature, vol. 2, pp. 823-26.
Ed. by Frank N. Magill. New York: Salem
Press, 1971.

1370. Collected Stories I. London and Melbourne: Mac-
millan & Company, Ltd., 1st ed., 1967.
New York: Alfred A. Knopf, Inc., 1968.
Toronto: Macmillan Company of Canada, Ltd., 1967.

Reviews of Collected Stories I

1371. Anonymous. Booklist 65 (15 September 1968): 103.

1372. _____. British Book News no. 331 (March 1968):238.

1373. _____. Kirkus Reviews 36 (15 April 1968): 484.

1374. Bannon, Barbara A. Publishers' Weekly 193 (15 April 1968):90.

1375. Cushman, Jerome. Library Journal 93 (1 June 1968):2261.

1376. Price, R. G. G. Punch 253 (29 November 1967):831.

1377. The Fanfarlo and Other Verse. Aldington, Ashford, and Kent, England: Hand & Flower Press, 1952.

Review of The Fanfarlo and Other Verse

1378. Treece, Henry. Poetry Quarterly [London] 14 (Autumn 1952):92-93.

1379. The Go-Away Bird and Other Stories. Harmondsworth, Middlesex, England: Penguin Books, Ltd., 1963. London: Macmillan & Company, Ltd., 1st ed., 1958. Philadelphia: J. B. Lippincott Company, 1960, hardbound; 1961 and 1974, paperback.

Translations of Stories from
The Go-Away Bird and Other Stories

1380. Der Seraph und der Sambesi und Andere Erzählungen. Trans. by Peter Naujack and Elisabeth Schnack. Zürich: Diogenes Verlag, 1963.

1381. Tachisare Tori. Trans. by Ebizuka Hiroshi. Tokyo: Sakai shoten, 1966.

1382. De Zwarte Madonna. Trans. by Johan van der Woude and Frans van der Woude. Amsterdam: Contact, 1970.

Reviews of The Go-Away Bird and Other Stories

1383. Anonymous. Booklist 57 (1 December 1960):
      211.

1384. _____ . Bookmark [New York State Library]
      20 (December 1960):67.

1385. _____ . British Book News no. 222 (Feb-
      ruary 1959):151.

1386. _____ . New Yorker 36 (12 November 1960):
      240.

1387. Burke, Herbert. Critic [Chicago] 19 (Decem-
      ber 1960-January 1961):62.

1388. Burnette, Frances. Library Journal 85 (15
      December 1960):4488.

1389. Grandsen, K. W. Encounter 65 (February
      1959):74-76.

1390. Hughes, Riley. Catholic World 192 (February
      1961):310.

1391. Lonergan, Joan. Catholic Library World 32
      (November 1960):140.

1392. McConkey, James. Epoch 10 (Fall 1960):249-
      51.

1393. Quinton, Anthony. London Magazine 6 (June
      1959):68-72.

1394. Memento Mori and The Ballad of Peckham Rye. New
      York: Modern Library, 1966.

1395. Memento Mori and The Girls of Slender Means. Lon-
      don: Reprint Society, 1965.

1396. A Muriel Spark Trio: The Comforters, The Ballad of
      Peckham Rye, Memento Mori. Philadelphia: J. B.
      Lippincott Company, 1962.

Review of A Muriel Spark Trio

1397. Hartley, Lois. America 107 (1 September 1962):675.

1398. Two by Muriel Spark: The Ballad of Peckham Rye and The Bachelors. New York: Dell Publishing Co., Delta Books, 1964, paperback.

1399. Voices at Play [Short Stories and Radio Plays]. London: Macmillan & Company, Ltd., 1st ed., 1961.
New York: St. Martin's Press, 1961.
Philadelphia: J. B. Lippincott Company, 1961, 1962.
Harmondsworth, Middlesex, England: Penguin Books, Ltd., 1966.
Toronto: The Copp Clark Company, 1961.

Reviews of Voices at Play

1400. Anonymous. Booklist 58 (15 June 1962):719-20.

1401. _____. British Book News no. 253 (September 1961):676.

1402. _____. Observer Weekend Review [London], 2 October 1966, p. 22.

1403. Burnette, Frances. Library Journal 87 (July 1962):2570.

1404. Feld, Rose. New York Herald Tribune Books, 6 May 1962, p. 6.

1405. Prescott, Orville. New York Times, 7 May 1962, p. 29.

1406. Singer, Burns. Listener 66 (13 July 1961):69.

1407. Young, B. A. Punch 241 (26 July 1961):152.

L. EDITED WORKS

1408.   The Brontë Letters. London and Melbourne: Macmillan & Company, Ltd., new edition, 1966.
London: Peter Nevill, Ltd., 1st ed., 1954.

1409.   The Letters of the Brontës. [Title of the American edition of The Brontë Letters.] Norman, Ok.: University of Oklahoma Press, 1954.

Reviews of The Brontë Letters/
Letters of the Brontës

1410.   Anonymous.   Booklist 51 (1 October 1954):61.

1411.   _____ . British Book News no. 168 (August 1954):455-56.

1412.   _____ . British Book News no. 316 (December 1966):935.

1413.   _____ . Times Literary Supplement [London], 25 June 1954, p. 414.

1414.   Blondell, J.   Etudes Anglaises 8 (1954):269-70.

1415.   Mary Shelley's The Last Man. London: Falcon Press, 1951. [In 1951 Muriel Spark did a radio broadcast on The Last Man, which was published under the title "Mary Shelley: a Prophetic Novelist" in Listener 45 (22 February 1951):305-306.   When Falcon Press was ready to publish in 1951 Mary Shelley's The Last Man with an Introduction by Muriel Spark, she requested that the book should not be published.   However, an abbreviated version of Muriel Spark's exposition of some passages from The Last Man is contained in the appendix to Child of Light and in a chapter of this book.   This information can be found in Derek Stanford's book Muriel Spark: A Biographical and Critical Study, p. 162.]

144

1416. Spark, Muriel, and Stanford, Derek, eds. Letters of
       John Henry Newman. [Introduction by Spark and Stan-
       ford.]
       London: Peter Owen, Ltd. , 1st ed. , 1957.
       Toronto: The Copp Clark Company, 1957.
       Westminister, Md. : Newman Press, 1957.

       Review of Letters of John Henry Newman

       1417. Zeno, Fr. O. F. M. Dublin Review (1957):369-
              73.

1418. Spark, Muriel, and Stanford, Derek, eds. My Best
       Mary: The Selected Letters of Mary Wollstonecraft
       Shelley.
       Folcroft, Pa. : Folcroft Library Editions, 1972, 1974.
       London: Allan Wingate, Ltd. , 1st ed. , 1953.
       New York: Roy Publishers, 1954.
       Philadelphia: Richard West, 1974.

       Reviews of My Best Mary

       1419. Anonymous. Listener 50 (23 July 1953):151-
              52.

       1420. _____. Manchester Guardian, 10 April
              1953, p. 4.

       1421. _____. New Yorker 30 (3 April 1954):116-
              17.

       1422. _____. Wisconsin Library Bulletin 50 (July-
              August 1954):178.

       1423. Reeves, James. Observer [London], 26 April
              1953, p. 9.

       1424. Willis, Katharine Tappert. Library Journal
              79 (15 March 1954):548-49.

1425. A Selection of Poems by Emily Brontë. [Introduction
       by Spark.] London: Grey Walls Press, Ltd. , 1952.
       London and New York: British Book Centre, 1953.
       [Title on front and back covers is Selected Poems of
       Emily Brontë.]

1426. Spark, Muriel, and Stanford, Derek. Tribute to

Wordsworth: A Miscellany of Opinion for the Centenary of the Poet's Death. [Foreword by Herbert Read, Introduction by Spark and Stanford.] Folcroft, Pa.: Folcroft Library Editions, 1974, hardbound reprint of 1950 edition.
London: Allan Wingate Ltd., 1st ed., 1950, and Theodore Brunn, limited deluxe edition, 1950.
Port Washington, N.Y.: Kennikat Press, Inc., 1970, 1974, hardbound reprint of 1950 edition.

Reviews of Tribute to Wordsworth

1427. Anonymous. Listener 43 (11 May 1950):843.

1428. Crane, Waldo. Poetry Review [London] 51 (September-October 1950):279-80.

1429. Hallowell, W. N. Poetry Review [London] 52 (January-February 1951):44-45.

1430. Wilcox, Stuart C. Books Abroad 25 (Winter 1951):174.

M.   WORKS TRANSLATED

1431. Spark, Muriel, and Stanford, Derek. Poems XVII from Shadows of My Love, by Guillaume Appollinaire. Poetry Quarterly [London] 12 (Autumn 1950):149.

PART IV

WRITINGS ABOUT
MURIEL SPARK

A. BOOKS

1432. Bergonzi, Bernard. The Situation of the Novel. London: Macmillan & Company, Ltd., and Pittsburgh: University of Pittsburgh Press, 1970, pp. 22, 75. [Memento Mori]

1433. Berthoff, Warner. Fictions and Events: Essays in Criticism and Literary History. New York: E. P. Dutton & Company, Inc., 1971, pp. 118-54. [The Mandelbaum Gate]

1434. Bradbury, Malcolm. Possibilities: Essays on the State of the Novel. London, Oxford, and New York: Oxford University Press, 1973, pp. 177-80, 247-50, 259. [The Driver's Seat, Memento Mori, Not to Disturb, The Public Image]

1435. Burgess, Anthony. The Novel Now: A Guide to Contemporary Fiction. New York: W. W. Norton & Company, Inc., 1967, pp. 127-29, 131. [The Ballad of Peckham Rye, The Comforters, The Girls of Slender Means, The Mandelbaum Gate, Memento Mori, The Prime of Miss Jean Brodie]

1436. Enright, Dennis J. Man Is an Onion: Reviews and Essays. London: Chatto & Windus, Ltd., 1972, and LaSalle, Ill.: Library Press/Open Court Publishing Co., 1973, pp. 32-38. [The Mandelbaum Gate]

1437. Fraser, George S. The Modern Writer and his World. London: Derek Verschoyle, 1953; Andre Deutsch Ltd., 1964; Penguin Books, Ltd., 1964. New York: Frederick A. Praeger, Inc., 1965, pp. 171-72. [On Spark's earlier novels.]

1438. Fricker, Robert. Der Moderne Englische Roman. Göttingen: Vandenhoeck & Ruprecht, 2 Aufl., 1966, p. 221. [The Bachelors, Memento Mori]

1439. Friedman, Melvin J., ed. The Vision Obscured:
       Perceptions of Some Twentieth-Century Catholic Nov-
       elists. New York: Fordham University Press, 1970,
       pp. 47, 48, 95-107. Reviewed by Vincent Ferrer
       Blehl in Thought 46 (1971):618-19. [The Bachelors,
       The Comforters, The Girls of Slender Means, The
       Mandelbaum Gate, Memento Mori, The Prime of Miss
       Jean Brodie]

1440. Humphries, Christmas, ed. Poems I Remember.
       London: Michael Joseph, 1960 [page unknown]. ["The
       Robe and the Song"]

1441. Ivask, Ivar, and von Wilpert, Gero, eds. World Lit-
       erature Since 1945. New York: Frederick Ungar Pub-
       lishing Co., 1973, pp. 107, 109-10. [The Bachelors,
       "The Ballad of the Fanfarlo," The Ballad of Peckham
       Rye, The Comforters, Doctors of Philosophy, The
       Girls of Slender Means, The Mandelbaum Gate, Me-
       mento Mori, The Prime of Miss Jean Brodie, The
       Public Image]

1442. Karl, Frederick R. A Reader's Guide to the Con-
       temporary English Novel. New York: Farrar, Straus
       & Giroux, rev. ed., 1972, pp. 207, 274, 280, 349-
       52. [The Bachelors, The Ballad of Peckham Rye, Col-
       lected Stories I, The Comforters, The Girls of Slender
       Means, The Mandelbaum Gate, Memento Mori, The
       Prime of Miss Jean Brodie, The Public Image, Robin-
       son]

1443. Kemp, Peter. Muriel Spark. London: Paul Elek
       Books Ltd., 1974, 167p. Reviewed by Gabriele Annan
       in Times Literary Supplement [London], 15 November
       1974, p. 1277. [Discussion of Spark's novels, except
       The Abbess of Crewe, along with these major essays:
       "The Brontës as Teachers," "The Desegregation of
       Art," "How I Became a Novelist," "My Conversion,"
       "The Mystery of Job's Suffering," "The Religion of an
       Agnostic," "Speaking of Writing--I," "What Images Re-
       turn." Short stories discussed: "Bang-Bang You're
       Dead," "The Curtain Blown by the Breeze," "The
       Fathers' Daughters," "The Go-Away Bird," The Porto-
       bello Road." These poems: "Conversations," "Day
       of Rest," "Faith and Works." These interviews: "In-
       terview with Malcolm Muggeridge," "Keeping It Short,"
       "Writers in the Tense Present."]

1444. Kermode, Frank. Continuities. [Chapter XXII: "Muriel Spark."] London: Routledge & Kegan Paul, Ltd., 1968, pp. 202-16. [Selected, formerly published reviews by Kermode of The Girls of Slender Means and The Mandelbaum Gate.]

1445. _____. Modern Essays. [Chapter XVII: "Muriel Spark."] London: William Collins, Sons & Co., Ltd., 1971, pp. 267-83. [Selected, formerly published reviews by Kermode of Spark's two novels cited in entry # 1444 and of The Public Image.]

1446. Kienzle, Siegfried. Modern World Theater. Trans. from the German by Alexander Henderson and Elizabeth Henderson. New York: Frederick Ungar Publishing Co., 1970, pp. 418-19. [The Ballad of Peckham Rye, Doctors of Philosophy]

1447. Kostelanetz, Richard, ed. On Contemporary Literature. Introduction by R. Kostelanetz. New York: Avon Books, expanded edition, 1969, pp. 591-96. [The Bachelors, The Ballad of Peckham Rye, The Comforters, The Girls of Slender Means, The Go-Away Bird, Memento Mori, The Prime of Miss Jean Brodie]

1448. Lodge, David. The Novelist at the Crossroads and Other Essays on Fiction and Criticism. Ithaca, N.Y.: Cornell University Press, and London: Routledge & Kegan Paul Ltd., 1971, pp. 24, 25, 119-44, 287-88. [The Comforters, The Prime of Miss Jean Brodie]

1449. Malin, Irvin, ed. Critical Views of Isaac Bashevis Singer. London: University of London Press, Ltd., and New York: New York University Press, 1969, pp. 149-68. [The Bachelors, The Ballad of Peckham Rye, The Comforters, The Mandelbaum Gate, Memento Mori, Robinson]

1450. Malkoff, Karl. Muriel Spark. Monograph--Columbia Essays on Modern Writers, No. 36. New York and London: Columbia University Press, 1968, 48p. Reviewed by Larry L. Dickson in Abstracts of English Studies 16 (September 1972):48, and by Frank McCombie in Notes and Queries 17 (1970):475-76. [The Bachelors, The Ballad of Peckham Rye, The Comforters, The Girls of Slender Means, The Mandelbaum

Gate, Memento Mori, The Prime of Miss Jean Brodie,
The Public Image, Robinson]

1451. Mannheimer, Monica. Pilot Book to Muriel Spark,
      The Go-Away Bird and Other Stories: Introduction and
      Commentary. Stockholm: Almqvist & Wiksell, 1970,
      37p. [Contains a short bibliography in English.]

1452. Raban, Jonathan. The Technique of Modern Fiction:
      Essays in Practical Criticism. London: Edward
      Arnold, Ltd., 1968, and Notre Dame, Ind.: Univer-
      sity of Notre Dame Press, 1969, p. 102. [The Ballad
      of Peckham Rye]

1453. Rhode, Eric, ed. Novelists' Theatre. Harmondsworth,
      Middlesex, England and Ringwood, Victoria, Australia:
      Penguin Books, Ltd., 1966, pp. 7-19. [Discussion of
      the relationship of Spark's novels, especially Doctors
      of Philosophy, to the theater.]

1454. Riley, Carolyn, and Harte, Barbara, eds. Contem-
      porary Literary Criticism. Vol. 2. Detroit: Gale
      Research Company, Book Tower, 1974, pp. 414-19.
      [Selections from reviews of Spark's novels.]

1455. Robson, W. W. Modern English Literature. London,
      Oxford, and New York: Oxford University Press,
      1970, p. 148. [The Prime of Miss Jean Brodie]

1456. Stanford, Derek. Muriel Spark: A Biographical and
      Critical Study. Bibliography by Bernard Stone. Font-
      well, Sussex, and London: Centaur Press Ltd., 1963,
      184p. Reviewed by Alan Denson in Books Abroad 38
      (Summer 1964):316-17, and in British Book News no.
      281 (January 1964):68. [A personal recollection which
      chronicles Spark's growth as a writer, with explanation
      of circumstances which stimulated a number of crea-
      tive and scholarly works, along with critical assess-
      ment of individual works.]

1457. Stubbs, Patricia. Muriel Spark. Monograph--Writers
      and Their Works. Harlow, Essex, England: Longman
      Group Ltd. (for the British Council), 1973; New York:
      British Book Center, 1974, 35p. Reviewed by A. R.
      Jacquette in Abstracts of English Studies 18 (Novem-
      ber 1974):182-83. [The Bachelors, The Ballad of
      Peckham Rye, The Comforters, Doctors of Philosophy,

The Driver's Seat, The Girls of Slender Means, The
Go-Away Bird, The Mandelbaum Gate, Memento Mori,
Not to Disturb, The Prime of Miss Jean Brodie, The
Public Image, Robinson]

1458. Swinden, Patrick. Unofficial Selves: Character in the
Novel from Dickens to the Present Day. New York:
Harper & Row, Publishers, Inc.; Barnes & Noble Book,
1973, pp. 221-30, 231, 256. [The Bachelors, The
Ballad of Peckham Rye, The Comforters, "A Curtain
Blown by the Breeze," "The Go-Away Bird," The
Mandelbaum Gate, Memento Mori, "Miss Pinkerton's
Apocalypse," Not to Disturb, "The Portobello Road,"
"The Seraph and the Zambesi"]

1459. Temple, Ruth Z., and Tucker, Martin, comps. and
eds. A Library of Literary Criticism: Modern
British Literature. Vol. 3. New York: Frederick
Ungar Publishing Co., 1966, 1967, pp. 163-65. [Se-
lections from reviews of Spark's novels.]

1460. Walker, Warren S., comp. Twentieth-Century Short
Story Explication. Hamden, Conn.: The Shoe String
Press, Inc., 1963, p. 112; 1967, pp. 606-607; 1970,
p. 228. [Bibliographic list of some of Spark's stories.]

B. DISSERTATIONS

1461. Keyser, Barbara Elizabeth Yarbrough. "The Dual
Vision of Muriel Spark. " Ph. D. dissertation. Tulane
University, 1971. [Abstract in Dissertation Abstracts
International 32 (January 1972):4005A.]

1462. Laffin, Gerry Starr. "Unresolved Dualities in the
Novels of Muriel Spark. " Ph. D. dissertation. The
University of Wisconsin, 1973. [Abstract in Disser-
tation Abstracts International 34 (January 1974):4268A.]

1463. Legris, Maurice Roger. "Muriel Spark's Use of the
Non-Material: Prolegomena to a Theological Critique. "
Ph. D. dissertation. University of Oregon, 1973.
[Abstract in Dissertation Abstracts International 34
(June 1974):7763A-64A.]

1464. McLeod, Patrick Gould. "Vision and the Moral Encounter: A Reading of Muriel Spark's Novels. " Ph. D.
dissertation. Rice University, 1973. [Abstract in
Dissertation Abstracts International 34 (September
1973):1286A-87A.]

1465. Mansfield, Joseph Gerald. "Another World Than This:
The Gothic and The Catholic in the Novels of Muriel
Spark. " Ph. D. dissertation. The University of Iowa,
1973. [Abstract in Dissertation Abstracts International
34 (March 1974):5980A.]

1466. Mobley, Jonnie Patricia. "Towards Logres: The
Operation of Efficacious Grace in Novels by C. S.
Lewis, Charles Williams, Muriel Spark, and Gabriel
Fielding. " Ph. D. dissertation. University of Southern
California, 1973. [Abstract in Dissertation Abstracts
International 34 (January 1974):4274A.]

1467. Quinn, Joseph Allan. "A Study of the Satiric Element
in the Novels of Muriel Spark. " Ph. D. dissertation.

Purdue University, 1969.   [Abstract in <u>Dissertation</u>
<u>Abstracts International</u> 30 (March 1970):<u>3954A.</u>]

C. CRITICAL ESSAYS

1468. Anonymous. "At Another Distance." Times Literary Supplement [London], 30 November 1967, p. 1125. [Collected Stories I]

1469. _____. "Confidence Trickster." Time 76 (14 November 1960):108, 110. [The Go-Away Bird]

1470. _____. "A Devil Called Douglas." Time 76 (15 August 1960):82. [The Ballad of Peckham Rye]

1471. _____. "Down the Up Staircase." Time 93 (7 March 1969):83, E9. [The Prime of Miss Jean Brodie]

1472. _____. "The Earlier Mr. Masefield." Times Literary Supplement [London], 11 September 1953, p. 578. [John Masefield]

1473. _____. "Emily Brontë." Times Literary Supplement [London], 20 November 1953, p. 739. [Emily Brontë: Her Life and Work]

1474. _____. "Faith and Fancy." Times Literary Supplement [London], 4 March 1960, p. 141. [The Ballad of Peckham Rye]

1475. _____. "Fiction of 1968: Muriel Spark: The Public Image." In T. L. S.: Essays and Reviews from the Times Literary Supplement 1968, vol. 7, pp. 71-73. [No editor given.] London, New York, and Toronto: Oxford University Press, 1969.

1476. _____. "Ghouls and Ghosts." Times Literary Supplement [London], 7 July 1961, p. 418. [Voices at Play]

1477. _____. "Hell in the Royal Borough." Times

Literary Supplement [London], 20 September 1963, p. 701. [The Girls of Slender Means]

1478. _____. "Hidden Depths." Newsweek 59 (22 January 1962):81. [The Prime of Miss Jean Brodie]

1479. _____. "Individual Voices." Times Literary Supplement [London], 2 January 1953, p. 6. [The Fanfarlo and Other Verse]

1480. _____. "Light and Shade in New Novels." Times Weekly Review [London], 10 March 1960, p. 17. [The Ballad of Peckham Rye]

1481. _____. "Living and Learning." Times Weekly Review [London], 6 July 1961, p. 10. [Voices at Play]

1482. _____. "Meal for a Masochist." Times Literary Supplement [London], 25 September 1970, p. 1074.

1483. _____. "The Mental Squint of Muriel Spark." The Sunday Times [London], 30 September 1962, p. 14.

1484. _____. "Mistress of Style." Times Literary Supplement [London], 3 November 1961, p. 785. [The Prime of Miss Jean Brodie]

1485. _____. "More than Female Savagery." Time 92 (1 November 1968):102.

1486. _____. "Novels of 1963: Muriel Spark: The Girls of Slender Means." In T. L. S.: Essays and Reviews from the Times Literary Supplement 1963, vol. 2, pp. 100-102. [No editor given.] London, New York, and Toronto: Oxford University Press, 1964.

1487. _____. "Novels of 1965: Muriel Spark: The Mandelbaum Gate." In T. L. S.: Essays and Reviews from the Times Literary Supplement 1965, vol. 4, pp. 34-36. [No editor given.] London, New York, and Toronto: Oxford University Press, 1966.

1488. _____. "Out of Eden." Time 82 (13 September 1963):114, 116. [The Girls of Slender Means]

1489. _____. "Portrait of Mary Shelley." Times Literary Supplement [London], 4 April 1952, p. 238. [Child of Light]

1490.   . "Profound Comedy. " Newsweek 62 (16 September 1963):91-92. [The Girls of Slender Means]

1491.   . "Public Entertainers. " Times Literary Supplement [London], 27 July 1962, p. 536. [John Masefield]

1492.   . "Questing Characters. " Times Literary Supplement [London], 22 February 1957, p. 109. [The Comforters]

1493.   . "Questions and Answers. " Times Literary Supplement [London], 27 June 1958, p. 357. [Robinson]

1494.   . "Reintroducing Newman. " Times Literary Supplement [London], 16 August 1957, p. 496. [Letters of John Henry Newman]

1495.   . "Rich Bitches. " Economist 246 (10 March 1973):118. [The Hothouse by the East River]

1496.   . "Salute of the Week: Maggie Smith. " Cue: Magazine for New York and Suburbs 38 (8 March 1969):1. [Observations about the star of the movie, "The Prime of Miss Jean Brodie. "]

1497.   . "Scrolls and Sideburns. " Newsweek 66 (18 October 1965):130-31. [The Mandelbaum Gate]

1498.   . "Sense and Sensibility. " Times Literary Supplement [London], 19 December 1958, p. 733. [The Go-Away Bird]

1499.   . "Shadow Boxing. " Times Literary Supplement [London], 2 March 1973, p. 229.

1500.   . "Shallowness Everywhere. " Times Literary Supplement [London], 13 June 1968, p. 612. [The Public Image]

1501.   . "Shelley and Mary. " Times Literary Supplement [London], 17 April 1953, p. 248. [My Best Mary]

1502.   . "Short Notices. " Time 77 (14 April 1961): 115. [The Bachelors]

1503. _____. "Speaking of Writing." Times [London], 21 November 1963, p. 18. [The Girls of Slender Means, Memento Mori]

1504. _____. "Stag Party." Times Literary Supplement [London], 14 October 1960, p. 657. [The Bachelors, The Ballad of Peckham Rye, Memento Mori]

1505. _____. "Talking about Jerusalem." Times Literary Supplement [London], 14 October 1965, p. 913. [The Mandelbaum Gate]

1506. _____. "Verse and Versatility." Times Literary Supplement [London], 15 February 1968, p. 155. [Collected Poems I]

1507. _____. "The Wordsworth Harvest." Times Literary Supplement [London], 16 June 1950, p. 375. [Tribute to Wordsworth]

1508. Ackroyd, Peter. "Sending Up." Spectator 233 (16 November 1974):634. [The Abbess of Crewe]

1509. Adler, Renata. "Muriel Spark." In On Contemporary Literature, pp. 591-96. Ed. by Richard Kostelanetz. New York: Avon Books, expanded edition, 1969. [The Bachelors, The Ballad of Peckham Rye, The Comforters, The Girls of Slender Means, The Go-Away Bird, Memento Mori, The Prime of Miss Jean Brodie]

1510. Allen, Bruce. Library Journal 97 (15 March 1972): 1034. [Not to Disturb]

1511. Allen, Walter. "New Short Stories." New Statesman 56 (20 December 1958):890. [The Ballad of Peckham Rye]

1512. _____. "The Possessed." New Statesman 60 (15 October 1960):580-81. [The Bachelors]

1513. Annan, Gabriele. "Holy Watergate." Times Literary Supplement [London], 15 November 1974, p. 1277. [The Abbess of Crewe]

1514. Armour, Richard. "Novel Spoofs, Analyzes Age." Los Angeles Times Book Reviews, 17 April 1960, p. V7. [Memento Mori]

1515. Bacon, Martha. "Very Neat, This Tale--Engaging, Too." New York Herald Tribune Book Review, 1 September 1957, p. 8. [The Comforters]

1516. Baldanza, Frank. "Muriel Spark and the Occult." Wisconsin Studies in Contemporary Literature 6 (Summer 1965):190-203. Also in Edward A. Kearns, Abstracts of English Studies 13 (February 1970):383. [The Comforters, The Girls of Slender Means]

1517. Balliett, Whitney. "Moses in the Old Brit'n." New Yorker 33 (18 January 1958):99-101. [The Comforters]

1518. Barnes, Clive. "Theater: Teacher's Tale." New York Times, 17 January 1968, p. 39. Also in New York Times Theater Reviews 1920-1970, v. 8/1967-1970, 17 January 1968 [pages are not numbered], and in New York Theatre Critics' Reviews 29 (week of 22 January 1968):381. ["The Prime of Miss Jean Brodie"]

1519. Baro, Gene. "Ladies in Waiting." New York Herald Tribune Book Week, 15 September 1963, p. 20. [The Girls of Slender Means]

1520. Bedford, Sybille. "Fantasy Without Whimsy." Saturday Review 43 (19 November 1960):28-29. [The Go-Away Bird]

1521. _____. "Frontier Regions." Spectator 215 (29 October 1965):555-56. [The Mandelbaum Gate]

1522. Bellasis, M. "Wind and Rainy." Tablet 220 (19 November 1966):1302-1303. [The Brontë Letters]

1523. Bentley, Phyllis. "Letters from Haworth." Listener 51 (20 May 1954):879-80. [The Brontë Letters]

1524. Berthoff, Warner. "Fortunes of the Novel: Muriel Spark and Iris Murdoch." Massachusetts Review 8 (Spring 1967):301-32. Also in Warner Berthoff, Fictions and Events: Essays in Criticism and Literary History, pp. 118-54. New York: E. P. Dutton & Company, Inc., 1971. Also in Robert L. Dial, Abstracts of English Studies 12 (May 1969):249. [The Comforters, John Masefield, The Mandelbaum Gate, Memento Mori]

1525. Birstein, Ann. "An Uncanny Aim. " Reporter 23 (10 November 1960):55. [The Go-Away Bird, Memento Mori]

1526. Blackburn, Tom. "The Poet as Craftsman. " Poetry Review [London] 59 (Spring 1968):57-58. [Collected Poems I]

1527. Bloom, Edward A. "Emily Brontë Dissected. " Saturday Review 37 (13 November 1954):34. [Emily Brontë: Her Life and Work]

1528. _____. "Shelley's Muse. " Saturday Review 37 (12 June 1954):17. [My Best Mary]

1529. Boucher, Anthony. "Criminals at Large. " New York Times Book Review, 19 October 1958, p. 59. [Robinson]

1530. Bradbury, Malcolm. "Muriel Spark's Fingernails. " Critical Quarterly [Manchester, England] 14 (Autumn 1972):241-50. Also in Malcolm Bradbury, Possibilities: Essays on the State of the Novel, pp. 247-55. London, Oxford, and New York: Oxford University Press, 1973. And in Fred Erisman, Abstracts of English Studies 17 (February 1974):384. [The Driver's Seat]

1531. _____. "A Pilgrim's Progress. " New York Times Book Review, 31 October 1965, pp. 4, 52. [The Mandelbaum Gate]

1532. Brendon, Piers. "Lucid Astringency. " Books and Bookmen 13 (July 1968):32. [The Public Image]

1533. Brickner, Richard P. "Three Novels: Nightmares, Conspirators, and Maniacs. " New York Times Book Review, 29 April 1973, pp. 24-25. [The Hothouse by the East River]

1534. Broyard, Anatole. "The Old Spark Is Missing. " New York Times, 29 March 1972, p. 41. [Not to Disturb]

1535. Bryden, Ronald. "Childe Colin. " Spectator 204 (4 March 1960):329. [The Ballad of Peckham Rye]

1536. Bullough, Geoffrey. "Chapter III: The Nineteenth Century and After, I. " In The Year's Work in English

Studies. Vols. 33 (1952) and 34 (1953). Ed. by
Frederick S. Boas and Beatrice White. London:
Geoffrey Cumberlege for Oxford University Press,
1954, 1955. [On Child of Light, vol. 33, p. 235; on
My Best Mary, vol. 34, pp. 258-59; on Emily Brontë:
Her Life and Works, vol. 34, pp. 270-71.]

1537. Butcher, Maryvonne. "Remembrance of Things Past."
Tablet [London] 217 (26 October 1963):1150. [The
Girls of Slender Means]

1538. Byatt, A. S. "Empty Shell." New Statesman 75 (14
June 1968):807-808. [The Public Image]

1539. _____. "Whittled and Spiky Art." New Statesman
74 (15 December 1967):848. Also in R. E. Wiehe, Abstracts of English Studies 11 (December 1968):531.
[Collected Poems I, Collected Stories I]

1540. Casson, Allan. "Muriel Spark's The Girls of Slender
Means." Critique: Studies in Modern Fiction 7
(Spring-Summer 1965):94-96. [The Girls of Slender
Means, The Prime of Miss Jean Brodie]

1541. Chapman, John. "Zoe Caldwell Superb in 'Prime of
Jean Brodie,' Unusual Play." New York Theatre
Critics' Reviews 29 (week of 22 January 1968):382.

1542. Clements, Robert J. "European Literary Scene."
Saturday Review 51 (3 August 1968):20. [The Public
Image]

1543. Cohen, Gerda L. "Tilting the Gate." Midstream
[New York] 12 (January 1966):68-70. [The Mandelbaum Gate]

1544. Cooke, Richard P. "The Theater: An Apple for the
Teacher." New York Theatre Critics' Reviews 29
(week of 22 January 1968):381-82. ["The Prime of
Miss Jean Brodie"]

1545. Crane, Milton. "Wit Honed to Biting Edge." Chicago
Tribune Magazine of Books, 15 September 1963, p. 5.
[The Girls of Slender Means]

1546. Crozier, Mary. "Voices in a Void." Manchester
Guardian Weekly, 17 August 1961, p. 11. [Voices at
Play]

1547. Cruttwell, Patrick. "Fiction Chronicle." Hudson Review 24 (Spring 1971):177-84. [The Driver's Seat]

1548. Cuffe, Edwin D. "Wimblegate? Watercloister?" Washington Post Book World, 17 November 1974, p. 1. [The Abbess of Crewe]

1549. Davenport, John. "Treachery in the Classroom." Observer Weekend Review [London], 29 October 1961, p. 30. [The Prime of Miss Jean Brodie]

1550. Davidson, Peter. "The Miracles of Muriel Spark." Atlantic Monthly 222 (October 1968):139-42. [Collected Poems I, Collected Stories I, The Public Image]

1551. De Lissovoy, Susan. "Living Was Writing." Reporter 36 (18 May 1967):40, 42. [Emily Brontë: Her Life and Work]

1552. De Mott, Benjamin. "In and Out of Storytown." Hudson Review 14 (Spring 1961):133-41. [The Go-Away Bird]

1553. Denniston, Robin. "All on Her Own." Time and Tide [London] 41 (29 October 1960):1309. [The Bachelors]

1554. Derrick, Christopher. "Human Research." Tablet [London] 214 (5 March 1960):229-30. [The Ballad of Peckham Rye]

1555. Dierickx, J. "A Devil-Figure in a Contemporary Setting: Muriel Spark's The Ballad of Peckham Rye." Revue des Langues Vivantes [Brussels] 33 (1967):576-87.

1556. Dobie, Ann B. "Muriel Spark's Definition of Reality." Critique: Studies in Modern Fiction 12 (December 1970):20-27. Also in A. C. Hoffman, Abstracts of English Studies 17 (October 1973):111.

1557. _____. "The Prime of Miss Jean Brodie: Muriel Spark Bridges the Credibility Gap." Arizona Quarterly 25 (Autumn 1969):217-28.

1558. Dobie, Ann B., and Wooton, Carl. "Spark and Waugh: Similarities by Coincidence." Midwest Quarterly [Pittsburg, Kansas] 13 (Summer 1972):423-34. Also in

Raymond C. Phillips, Abstracts of English Studies 16
(June 1973):655. [Comparison of Spark's The Comforters with Waugh's The Ordeal of Gilbert Pinfold.]

1559. Dolbier, Maurice. "Muriel Spark's Middle East."
New York Herald Tribune, 18 October 1965, p. 25.
[The Mandelbaum Gate]

1560. Downer, Alan S. "Old, New, Borrowed, and (a
Trifle) Blue: Notes on the New York Theatre, 1967-
1968." Quarterly Journal of Speech 54 (October 1968):
199-211. [The Prime of Miss Jean Brodie]

1561. Drescher, Horst W. "British Literature." In World
Literature Since 1945, pp. 65-121. Ed. by Ivar
Ivask and Gero von Wilpert. New York: Frederick
Ungar Publishing Co., 1973. [On Spark's novels,
pp. 107, 109-10.]

1562. Duffy, Martha. "A Whydunnit in Q-Sharp Major."
Time 96 (26 October 1970):119. [The Driver's Seat]

1563. Ellman, Mary. "The Problem of Elsa." New Statesman 85 (2 March 1973):308. [The Hothouse by the
East River]

1564. Engelborghs, Maurits. "Britse 'Lady Novelists.'"
Dietsche Warande en Belfort [Antwerp] no. 4 (1969):
286-92.

1565. _____. "Een Ongewone Engelse Roman." Kul-
tuurleven 27 (February 1960):140-42. Also in S. J.
Sackett, Abstracts of English Studies 3 (September
1960):396. [Memento Mori]

1566. Enright, Dennis J. "Public Doctrine and Private
Judging: Muriel Spark." New Statesman 70 (15 Oc-
tober 1965):563, 566. Also in Dennis J. Enright,
Man Is an Onion: Reviews and Essays, pp. 32-38.
London: Chatto & Windus, Ltd., 1972, and La Salle,
Ill.: Library Press/Open Court Publishing Company,
1973. [The Mandelbaum Gate]

1567. Evans, Illtud. "Crossing-Point." Tablet [London]
219 (23 October 1965):1184-85. [The Mandelbaum
Gate

1568. Evans, Robert O. "A Perspective for American

Novelists." Topic: A Journal of the Liberal Arts 6
(Fall 1966):58-66. Also in William V. Davis, Ab-
stracts of English Studies 11 (October 1968):439. [The
Mandelbaum Gate]

1569. Fallowell, Duncan. "Hothouse Madness." Books and
Bookmen 18 (April 1973):101. [The Hothouse by the
East River]

1570. Faÿ, Bernard. "Muriel Spark En Sa Fleur." La
Nouvelle Revue Française 14 (February 1966):307-15.
Also in Patricia Crunden, Abstracts of English Studies
11 (November 1968):486-87. [The Ballad of Peckham
Rye, The Comforters, The Girls of Slender Means,
Memento Mori, The Prime of Miss Jean Brodie]

1571. Feinstein, Elaine. "Loneliness Is Cold." London
Magazine n. s. 11 (February-March 1972):177-80.
[Not to Disturb]

1572. Ferguson, DeLancey. "In Their Own Words." New
York Times Book Review, 12 September 1954, p. 29.
[The Letters of the Brontës]

1573. Flint, R. W. "Prime Time in Edinburgh." New Republic 146 (29 January 1962):17, 20. [The Prime of
Miss Jean Brodie]

1574. Foote, Timothy. "Ars Moriendi." Time 101 (23
April 1973):100. [The Hothouse by the East River]

1575. Frakes, J. R. "Mock-Mod-Gothic." Chicago Tribune
and Washington Post Book World, 16 April 1972, p. 4.
[Not to Disturb]

1576. Frankel, Haskel. "The Ghostly Deus ex Machina."
Saturday Review 45 (2 June 1962):35. [Voices at
Play]

1577. _____. "Grub Street Gothic." Times Literary
Supplement [London], 12 November 1971, p. 1409.
[Not to Disturb]

1578. _____. "Spring Cleaning." Time 99 (17 April
1972):92. [Not to Disturb]

1579. Fraser, R. A. "A Contradiction--And a Comedy."

San Francisco Chronicle This World, 7 August 1960,
p. 19. [The Ballad of Peckham Rye]

1580. Fremont-Smith, Eliot. "Between the Two Jerusalems."
New York Times, 18 October 1965, p. 33. [The
Mandelbaum Gate]

1581. Fuller, John. "Jacqueline and Co." New Statesman
78 (31 October 1969):626, 628. [The Very Fine Clock]

1582. Gable, Sister Mariella. "Prose Satire and the Modern
Christian Temper." American Benedictine Review 11
(March-June 1960):29-30, 33. [Memento Mori]

1583. Gellert, Roger. "Pitiable Objects." New Statesman
64 (12 October 1962):501-502. [Doctors of Philosophy]

1584. Gilliatt, Penelope. "Black Laughs." Spectator 205
(21 October 1960):620-21. [The Bachelors, The Comforters, Memento Mori]

1585. Glendinning, Victoria. "Spark Plug." New Statesman
88 (22 November 1974):749. [The Abbess of Crewe]

1586. Graude, Luke. "Gabriel Fielding, New Master of the
Catholic Classic." Catholic World 197 (May 1963):
120-25. Also in Charles F. Wheeler, Abstracts of
English Studies 7 (November 1964):474. [Spark is one
of the recent Catholic novelists who have done well.]

1587. Graver, Lawrence. "Attending the Casseroles and a
Suicidal Baron." New York Times Book Review, 26
March 1972, pp. 6, 34-35. [Not to Disturb]

1588. Greeley, Andrew M. "Divine Spark." Reporter 34
(24 March 1966):56-58. [The Mandelbaum Gate]

1589. Green, Lois Wagner. "Wiles of Wee Dougie." Saturday Review 43 (30 July 1960):18. [The Ballad of
Peckham Rye]

1590. Greene, George. "Compulsion to Love." Kenyon
Review 31 (February 1969):267-72. [The Bachelors,
Collected Stories I, The Go-Away Bird, Memento
Mori]

1591. _____. "A Reading of Muriel Spark." Thought
43 (Autumn 1968):393-407.

1592. Grigson, Geoffrey. "Gods, Graves and Gold." <u>New</u>
<u>Statesman</u> 63 (4 May 1962):647-48. [John Mase-
field]

1593. Gross, John. "Passionate Pilgrimage." <u>New York</u>
<u>Review of Books</u> 5 (28 October 1965):12-15. [<u>The</u>
<u>Mandelbaum Gate</u>]

1594. Grosskurth, Phyllis. "The World of Muriel Spark:
Spirits or Spooks?" <u>Tamarack Review</u> [Toronto] no.
39 (Spring 1966):62-67. Also in T. O. Mallory, Ab-
<u>stracts of English Studies</u> 11 (May 1968):269. [Spark,
due to her conversion to Catholicism, "sees religion
as the central fact, and the supernatural as the basic
reality, of existence," as she shows in <u>The Mandel-</u>
<u>baum Gate</u> and <u>Memento Mori.</u>]

1595. Grosvenor, Peter. "In Search of Her Own Killer."
<u>Daily Express</u> [London], 24 September 1970, p. 12.
[<u>The Driver's Seat</u>]

1596. _____. "Mrs. Spark Makes Her Big Breakthrough--
to the Paperback Millions." <u>Daily Express</u> [London],
25 April 1963, p. 17. [<u>The Ballad of Peckham Rye</u>,
<u>The Bachelors</u>, <u>The Comforters</u>]

1597. Haney, R. W. "The Butler Won't Do It." <u>Christian</u>
<u>Science Monitor</u>, 20 April 1972, p. 13. [<u>Not to Dis-</u>
<u>turb</u>]

1598. Hart, Francis R. "Region, Character, and Identity in
Recent Scottish Fiction." <u>Virginia Quarterly Review</u>
43 (Autumn 1967):597-613. [On <u>The Prime of Miss</u>
<u>Jean Brodie</u>, pp. 601, 607-710.]

1599. Hartley, Anthony. "The Way We Live Now." <u>En-</u>
<u>counter</u> 15 (December 1960):80, 82. [<u>The Bachelors</u>]

1600. Hazzard, Shirley. "A Mind Like a Blade." <u>New</u>
<u>York Times Book Review</u>, 29 September 1968, pp. 1,
62. [<u>Collected Stories I</u>, p. 1; <u>The Public Image</u>,
p. 62.]

1601. Hengist, Philip. "Muriel Spark." <u>Punch</u> 245 (31 July
1963):175-76. [<u>The Bachelors</u>, <u>The Ballad of Peck-</u>
<u>ham Rye</u>, <u>The Comforters</u>, <u>Doctors of Philosophy</u>,
<u>The Go-Away Bird</u>, <u>Memento Mori</u>]

1602. Heppenstall, Rayner. "More about Wordsworth."
New Statesman and Nation 40 (1 July 1950):17. [Tribute to Wordsworth]

1603. Hicks, Granville. "A Hard Journey to Jordan."
Saturday Review 48 (16 October 1965):43-44. [The Mandelbaum Gate]

1604. _____. "Life Began in the Forties." Saturday Review 46 (14 September 1963):33-34. [The Girls of Slender Means]

1605. _____. "Treachery and the Teacher." Saturday Review 45 (20 January 1962):18. [The Prime of Miss Jean Brodie]

1606. Hodgart, Matthew. "Models of Mischief." New Statesman 61 (30 June 1961):1053. [Voices at Play]

1607. Hodgart, Patricia. Manchester Guardian, 12 February 1957, p. 4. [The Comforters]

1608. Hogan, William. San Francisco Chronicle This World, 4 February 1962, p. 28. [The Prime of Miss Jean Brodie]

1609. Holland, Mary. "The Prime of Muriel Spark." Observer Colour Supplement [London], 17 October 1965, pp. 8-10.

1610. Hollander, John. "Plain and Fancy: Notes on Four Novels." Yale Review 50 (September 1960):149, 153-54. [Giuseppe di Lampedusa's The Leopard, William Styron's Set this House on Fire, Muriel Spark's The Ballad of Peckham Rye, Wright Morris' Ceremony at Lone Tree]

1611. Hollowell, W. W. "Letter to the Editor." Poetry Review [London] 42 (January-February 1951):44-45. [Tribute to Wordsworth]

1612. Hope, Francis. "Mrs. Spark in Rome." Observer [London], 16 June 1968, p. 24. [The Public Image]

1613. Howard, Jane. "Muriel Spark: Mistress of Prim Skulduggery." Life 59 (22 October 1965):12, 15. [The Mandelbaum Gate]

1614. Howes, Barbara. "Three Women Writers." Massachusetts Review 5 (Spring 1964):583-86. [On Doris Lessing's A Man and Two Women and Other Stories, Mary McCarthy's The Group, and Muriel Spark's The Girls of Slender Means.]

1615. Hoyt, Charles Alva. "Muriel Spark: The Surrealist Jane Austen." In Contemporary British Novelists, pp. 125-43. Ed. by Charles Shapiro. Carbondale, Ill.: Southern Illinois University Press, 1965.

1616. Hughes, Riley. "Happy Malice." Renascence 14 (Autumn 1961):49-51. [The Bachelors, Robinson]

1617. Hutchens, John K. "The Bachelors." New York Herald Tribune, 1 March 1961, p. 21. [The Bachelors]

1618. _____. "Prime of Miss Jean Brodie." New York Herald Tribune, 17 January 1962, p. 23.

1619. Hynes, Samuel. "In the Great Tradition: The Prime of Muriel Spark." Commonweal 75 (23 February 1962):562-63, 567-68. Also in Bernard Farragher, Abstracts of English Studies 6 (February 1963):50. [The Bachelors, The Ballad of Peckham Rye, Memento Mori, The Prime of Miss Jean Brodie]

1620. _____. "A Minor Spark." Commonweal 76 (8 June 1962):285-86. [Voices at Play]

1621. Igoe, W. J. "Ironic Parable Exploiting the Edinburgh Spirit." Chicago Tribune Magazine of Books, 21 January 1962, p. 3. [The Prime of Miss Jean Brodie]

1622. Jacobsen, Josephine. "A Catholic Quartet." Christian Scholar 47 (Summer 1964):139-54. Also in A. G. Newell, Abstracts of English Studies 8 (January 1965): 5. [Spark reveals her Catholicism through her novels, as do Graham Greene, J. F. Powers, and Flannery O'Connor.]

1623. Janeway, Elizabeth. "A Changing Spark." Holiday 38 (September 1965):126-28. [The Mandelbaum Gate]

1624. Jelliffe, R. A. "Plays for the Outer Ear, Stories for the Inner." Chicago Tribune Magazine of Books, 13 May 1962, p. 4. [Voices at Play]

1625. Johnson, Lucy. "Split Personality." Progressive
       [Madison, Wis.] 28 (January 1964):50-51. [The Girls
       of Slender Means, Memento Mori]

1626. Jones, D. A. N. "Divided Selves." New York Re-
       view of Books 15 (22 October 1970):38, 40. [The
       Driver's Seat]

1627. Kermode, Frank. "Antimartyr." Listener 79 (13
       June 1968):778-79. [The Public Image]

1628. _____. "The British Novel Lives." Atlantic
       Monthly 230 (July 1972):85-88. [The Comforters, The
       Driver's Seat, The Mandelbaum Gate, Not to Disturb,
       The Public Image]

1629. _____. "Foreseeing the Unforeseen." Listener
       86 (11 November 1971):657-58. [Not to Disturb]

1630. _____. "God's Plots." Listener 78 (7 December
       1967):759-60. [Collected Poems I, Collected Stories
       I]

1631. _____. "The Novel as Jerusalem--Muriel Spark's
       Mandelbaum Gate." Atlantic Monthly 216 (October
       1965):92-94, 97-98. Also in Frank Kermode, Con-
       tinuities, pp. 207-16. London: Routledge & Kegan
       Paul, Ltd., 1968.

1632. _____. "The Prime of Miss Muriel Spark." New
       Statesman 66 (27 September 1963):397-98. Also in
       R. E. Wiehe, Abstracts of English Studies 7 (May
       1964):223. [The Bachelors, The Ballad of Peckham
       Rye, The Comforters, The Girls of Slender Means,
       Memento Mori, The Prime of Miss Jean Brodie]

1633. _____. "Sheerer Spark." Listener 84 (24 Septem-
       ber 1970):425-27. [The Driver's Seat]

1634. _____. "To The Girls of Slender Means." In
       Frank Kermode, Continuities, pp. 202-207. London:
       Routledge & Kegan Paul, Ltd., 1968.

1635. Kerr, Walter. "Behold Miss Brodie's Bravura."
       New York Theatre Critics' Reviews 29 (week of 29
       January 1968):376. ["The Prime of Miss Jean
       Brodie"]

1636. Kiely, R. "Brontë--Double-Teamed. " Christian
       Science Monitor, 13 October 1966, p. 4. [Emily
       Brontë: Her Life and Work]

1637. _____. "A Novel Snaps the Camera. " Christian
       Science Monitor, 14 November 1968, p. 15. [The
       Public Image]

1638. King, Francis. "Two Plain, One Pearl. " Time and
       Tide [London] 42 (2 November 1961):1845. [The
       Prime of Miss Jean Brodie]

1639. Kirgo, George. "Stories Good to Read. " Chicago
       Tribune Magazine of Books, 1 January 1961, Part 4,
       p. 6. [The Go-Away Bird]

1640. Knight, Arthur. "A Very Prime Miss Brodie. "
       Saturday Review 52 (8 March 1969):36. [Review of
       the movie "The Prime of Miss Jean Brodie. "]

1641. Kriegel, Leonard. "Muriel Spark in Jerusalem. "
       Commonweal 83 (14 January 1966):446, 448. [The
       Mandelbaum Gate]

1642. Laffin, Garry S. "Muriel Spark's Portrait of the
       Artist as a Young Girl. " Renascence 24 (1972):213-
       23.

1643. Lanning, George. "Silver Fish in the Plumbing. "
       Kenyon Review 23 (Winter 1961):173-75, 177-78. [The
       Ballad of Peckham Rye]

1644. Lerner, Max. "Elizabeth Taylor: What Does She
       Want Now?" McCall's 102 (June 1975):22-28. [Dis-
       cussion of the movie "The Driver's Seat, " p. 26.]

1645. Levin, Martin. "Spritely Tale. " Saturday Review
       40 (31 August 1957):25-26. [The Comforters]

1646. Lewis, Naomi. "A Sea Coast in Bohemia. " New
       Statesman and Nation 45 (30 May 1953):648, 650.
       [My Best Mary]

1647. Lindermann, Deborah. "Three English Novels. " Na-
       tion 211 (5 October 1970):312-14. [The Driver's Seat,
       by Muriel Spark; The Green Man, by Kingsley Amis;
       A Winter in the Hills, by John Wain.]

1648. Lister, Richard. "Trouble in the Class When the
       Teacher Like this Gets to Work." Evening Standard
       [London], 31 October 1961, p. 17. [The Prime of
       Miss Jean Brodie]

1649. Lodge, David. "Human Predicaments." Tablet [Lon-
       don] 215 (11 November 1961):1083-84. [The Prime of
       Miss Jean Brodie]

1650. _____. "Passing the Test." Tablet [London] 224
       (10 October 1970):978. [The Driver's Seat]

1651. _____. "The Uses and Abuses of Omniscience:
       Method and Meaning in Muriel Spark's The Prime of
       Miss Jean Brodie." Critical Quarterly [Manchester,
       England] 12 (1970):235-57. Also in David Lodge, The
       Novelist at the Crossroads, and Other Essays on Fic-
       tion and Criticism, pp. 119-44. Ithaca, N.Y.: Cor-
       nell University Press, 1971.

1652. _____. "Various Vocations." Tablet [London] 214
       (17 December 1960):1175-76. [The Bachelors]

1653. McDonnell, Thomas P. "Spinster's Progress."
       Critic [Chicago] 24 (December 1965-January 1966):79-
       80. [The Mandelbaum Gate]

1654. McDowell, Frederick P. W. "Recent British Fiction:
       Some Established Writers." Contemporary Literature
       11 (Summer 1970):401, 412. [The Public Image]

1655. _____. "Time of Plenty: Recent British Novels."
       Contemporary Literature 13 (Summer 1972):361, 387.

1656. McLaughlin, Richard. "Witty Novel by Muriel Spark
       Is Set in Housing Projects of English White-Collar
       Workers." Springfield Republican [Springfield, Mass.],
       11 September 1960, p. 5D. [The Ballad of Peckham
       Rye]

1657. Maddocks, Melvin. "The Spark Flair for Well-Bred
       Demonology." Life 65 (11 October 1968):10. [The
       Public Image]

1658. Malin, Irving. "The Deceptions of Muriel Spark."
       In The Vision Obscured, pp. 95-107. Ed. by Melvin
       J. Friedman. New York: Fordham University Press,

1970. [The Bachelors, pp. 100-101; The Comforters,
pp. 97-98, 102; The Girls of Slender Means, pp. 104-
105; The Mandelbaum Gate, pp. 96, 105-107; Memento
Mori, pp. 96, 99-100; The Prime of Miss Jean Brodie,
pp. 102-103.]

1659.   Malkoff, Karl. "Demonology and Dualism: The Supernatural in Isaac Singer and Muriel Spark." In Critical
Views of Isaac Bashevis Singer, pp. 149-68. Ed. by
Irvin Malin. New York: New York University Press,
1969.

1660.   Maloff, Saul. "The Contemporary British Comic
Novel: Satiric Eyes on a 'Revolution-of-Sorts.'"
Saturday Review 44 (8 April 1961):26. [The Bachelors]

1661.   _____. "Lady-Tiger." Newsweek 72 (21 October
1968):108, 110. [The Public Image]

1662.   Malpede, Karen. "A Two-Line Personal." New
Leader [New York] 53 (30 November 1970):20-21.
[The Driver's Seat]

1663.   Mano, D. Keith. "When They Are Good...." National
Review 24 (9 June 1972):646-47. [Not to Disturb]

1664.   Marks, Jason. "Book Trials: An Experiment in
Learning." CEA Forum 3 (October 1972):4-5. Also
in Bobbie J. Miller, Abstracts of English Studies 17
(December 1973):210. [The Prime of Miss Jean
Brodie]

1665.   Maura, Sister M. "Note from a Short Story." Critic
[Chicago] 20 (October-November 1961]:23. [A poem in-
spired by Spark's short story, "The Black Madonna."]

1666.   Maurer, Robert. "Art Imitates Life Imitating Art."
Saturday Review 51 (5 October 1968):31-32. [Collected
Stories I]

1667.   May, Derwent. "Holy Outrage." Listener 89 (1
March 1973):283-84. [The Hothouse by the East
River]

1668.   Mayne, Richard. "Fiery Particle--On Muriel Spark."
Encounter 25 (December 1965):61-62, 64, 66, 68.
Also in Lawrence R. Dawson, Jr., Abstracts of

English Studies 9 (September 1966):428. [The Bache-
lors, The Ballad of Peckham Rye, The Comforters,
Doctors of Philosophy, The Girls of Slender Means,
The Go-Away Bird, The Mandelbaum Gate, Memento
Mori, The Prime of Miss Jean Brodie, Robinson,
Voices at Play]

1669. Meath, Gerard. "Shelley's Wife." Tablet [London]
       201 (6 June 1953):494. [My Best Mary]

1670. Melik, Peter. "Modern Vocations." National Review
       10 (8 April 1961):221-22. [The Bachelors]

1671. Miller, Karl. "Among the Heathen." Observer [Lon-
       don], 26 November 1967, p. 27. [Collected Poems
       I, Collected Stories I]

1672. _____. "Hard Falls." New Statesman 62 (3 Novem-
       ber 1961):662-63. [Spark's The Prime of Miss Jean
       Brodie and Murdoch's A Severed Head]

1673. _____. "The Sisterhood." New York Review of
       Books 18 (20 April 1972):19-21. [Not to Disturb]

1674. Moynahan, Julian. "An Expert Pick of the Pack."
       New York Times Book Review, 5 December 1965, p.
       4. [The Mandelbaum Gate]

1675. Mudrick, Marvin. "Something to Say." Hudson Re-
       view 14 (Summer 1961):284-94. [The Bachelors]

1676. Murphy, Carol. "A Spark of the Supernatural." Ap-
       proach no. 60 (Summer 1966):26-30. Also in William
       K. Bottorff, Abstracts of English Studies 10 (June
       1967):342. [The Comforters, The Mandelbaum Gate,
       Memento Mori]

1677. Mutalik-Desai, A. A. "Doctors of Philosophy, A
       Play by Muriel Spark: A Review." Parashuramian
       [Parashurambhau College, India] [no vol.] (March
       1964):56-60.

1678. Nye, Robert. "Sparkling Spark." Manchester Guard-
       ian Weekly, 23 November 1974, p. 22. [The Abbess
       of Crewe]

1679. O'Faolain, Sean. "A Liberal Tory?" Spectator

199 (5 July 1957):21. [Letters of John Henry New-man]

1680. Ohmann, Carol B. "Muriel Spark's Robinson."
Critique: Studies in Modern Fiction 8 (Fall 1965):70-84.

1681. Ostermann, Robert. "The Public Image Makes Its
Point by Understatement." National Observer, 9
September 1969, p. B7. [Collected Stories I, The
Public Image]

1682. _____ . "In a Spark Parable, Little Is as It
Seems." National Observer, 2 June 1973, p. 21.
[The Hothouse by the East River]

1683. Pendennis. "Table Talk by Pendennis." Observer
[London], 23 December 1951, p. 5. [About Spark's
prize-winning short story, "The Seraph and the Zam-besi."]

1684. Pérez Minik, Domingo. "De lo Espeluznante a la
Alegoria." Insula 27 (February 1972):7.

1685. Peterson, Virginia. "Few Were More Delightful,
Lovely or Savage." New York Times Book Review,
15 September 1963, pp. 4-5. [The Girls of Slender
Means]

1686. Phelps, Robert. "As Narrative or Parable, It
Sparkles." New York Herald Tribune Books, 21
January 1962, p. 5. [The Prime of Miss Jean
Brodie]

1687. _____ . "The Devil's at Work Around the Clock."
New York Herald Tribune Book Review, 13 November
1960, p. 5. [The Go-Away Bird]

1688. _____ . "Muriel Spark's New One Sparkles."
New York Herald Tribune The Lively Arts and Book
Review, 5 March 1961, p. 28. [The Bachelors]

1689. _____ . "With a Happy Touch of the Brimstone."
New York Herald Tribune Book Review, 7 August
1960, p. 3. [The Ballad of Peckham Rye]

1690. Pickrel, Paul. "Some Odder Hands." Harper's

176 Muriel Spark

Magazine 224 (February 1962):105-106. [The Bachelors, The Prime of Miss Jean Brodie]

1691. Pippett, Aileen. "Aunt Louisa's Secret." New York
Times Book Review, 1 September 1957, p. 16. [The
Comforters]

1692. _____. "Continuations and Beginnings." Times
Literary Supplement [London], 4 December 1969,
p. 1389. [The Very Fine Clock]

1693. _____. "Salvation and Hocus Pocus Are All Very
Real." New York Times Book Review, 30 October
1960, p. 4. [The Go-Away Bird]

1694. Poore, Charles. "Wars Between Sexes." New York
Times, 24 October 1968, p. 45. [The Public Image]

1695. Potter, Nancy A. J. "Muriel Spark: Transformer of
the Commonplace." Renascence 17 (Spring 1965):115-
20. Also in Albert Misseldine, Abstracts of English
Studies 8 (December 1965):593. ["Transformation of
the unspectacular and commonplace into a parable of
good and evil" is a distinguishing feature of Spark's
novels.]

1696. Prescott, Orville. "Immaculate Professional Polish."
New York Times, 20 September 1963, p. 31. [The
Girls of Slender Means]

1697. Prescott, Peter S. "Novels: An Early Harvest."
Newsweek 84 (11 November 1974):110. [The Abbess
of Crewe]

1698. Price, Martin. "Believers: Some Recent Fiction."
Yale Review 63 (October 1973):80, 83-84, 86. [The
Hothouse by the East River]

1699. _____. "The Difficulties of Commitment: Some
Recent Novels." Yale Review 48 (June 1959):595,
597-98. [Memento Mori]

1700. _____. "In the Fielding Country: Some Recent
Fiction." Yale Review 47 (Autumn 1957):143, 148-50,
156. [The Comforters]

1701. _____. "Reason and Its Alternatives: Some

Recent Fiction. "   Yale Review 58 (Spring 1969):464,
469-70.   [The Public Image]

1702. _____. "The Self-Deceivers: Some Recent Fiction. " Yale Review 48 (December 1958):272, 277-79.
[Robinson]

1703. _____. "Splendid but Destructive Egotism. " New
York Times Book Review, 21 January 1962, p. 5.
[The Prime of Miss Jean Brodie]

1704. Prichard, William H. "Novel, Sex and Violence. "
Hudson Review 28 (Spring 1975):153. [The Abbess
of Crewe]

1705. Pryce-Jones, Alan. "Doubts about the Human Race. "
New York Herald Tribune, 5 October 1963, p. 7.
[The Girls of Slender Means]

1706. Quigly, Isabel. "Like It or Lump It. " Tablet [Lon-
don] 23 (30 December 1967):1344. [Collected Stories
I]

1707. _____. "Strong and Outspoken. " Spectator 218
(13 January 1967):49. [The Brontë Letters]

1708. Raban, Jonathan. "On Losing the Rabbit. " Encounter
40 (May 1973):80-85. [The Driver's Seat, The Hothouse by the East River, Not to Disturb]

1709. _____. "Vague Scriptures. " New Statesman 82
(12 November 1971):657-58. [The Driver's Seat, Not
to Disturb]

1710. Ramsaur, Hugh Wilgus. "The Premium Editor's Re-
port [of Prize Winning Poems]. " Poetry Review [Lon-
don] 38 (January-February 1947):79-88. [Critique of
"The Well"]

1711. Ratchford, Fannie. "Spark and Stanford's Emily
Brontë. " Nineteenth-Century Fiction 9 (September
1954):140-45. [Emily Brontë: Her Life and Work]

1712. Raven, Simon. "Heavens Below. " Spectator 211 (20
September 1963):354. Also in Robert Yackshaw, Ab-
stracts of English Studies 7 (April 1964):183. [The
Girls of Slender Means]

1713.   _____. "Somewhere in Europe." Spectator 200
           (27 June 1958):848. [Robinson]

1714. Raymond, John. "More about John Henry." New
       Statesman 54 (6 July 1957):27-28. [Letters of John
       Henry Newman]

1715. Reed, Douglas. "Taking Cocktails with Life." Books
       and Bookmen 16 (August 1971):10-14. Also in William
       D. Wolf, Abstracts of English Studies 16 (January
       1973):319. [The Ballad of Peckham Rye, The Com-
       forters, The Driver's Seat, The Mandelbaum Gate,
       Memento Mori, The Prime of Miss Jean Brodie,
       Robinson]

1716. Reid, Alexander. "The Novels of Muriel Spark."
       Scotland's Magazine 57 (April 1961):55-56.

1717. Reinhold, H. A. "Not So Harmless." Commonweal
       66 (23 August 1957):526-27. [The Comforters]

1718. Rhode, Eric. "The Novelist and the Theatre, [Intro-
       duction]." In Eric Rhode, Novelists' Theatre, pp. 7-
       19. Harmondsworth, Middlesex, England and Ringwood,
       Victoria, Australia: Penguin Books, Ltd., 1966. [Dis-
       cussion of Spark's play, "Doctors of Philosophy" and
       her first novel, The Comforters, in relation to the
       theater, pp. 17-19.]

1719. Richmond, Velma Bourgeois. "The Darkening Vision
       of Muriel Spark." Critique: Studies in Modern Fic-
       tion 15 (1973):71-85.

1720. Ricks, Christopher. "Extreme Instances." New York
       Review of Books 11 (19 December 1968):31-32. [Col-
       lected Poems I, Collected Stories I, The Public Image]

1721. Ridley, Clifford A. "Spark and Tyler Are Proof Anew
       of Knopf Knowledge of Top Fiction." National Ob-
       server, 29 November 1965, p. 25. [The Mandelbaum
       Gate]

1722. Robinson, James K. "An Author Revisited." Chicago
       Tribune Books Today, 25 September 1966, pp. 10-11.
       [Emily Brontë: Her Life and Work]

1723. Rogers, Thomas. "The Enchanted Void." Com-

mentary 31 (March 1961):268-70.   Also in Sven Eric
Molin, Abstracts of English Studies 4 (May 1961):180.
[The Ballad of Peckham Rye, The Comforters, The
Go-Away Bird, Memento Mori]

1724. Romijn Meijer, Henk. "Het Satirische Talent van
       Muriel Spark. " Tirade 6 (1962):157-69.

1725. Rosenthal, T. G. "The Death of Fiction. " New
       Statesman 85 (22 March 1968):389. Also in R. E.
       Wiehe, Abstracts of English Studies 11 (December
       1968):533. [It seems unlikely that fiction is really
       dying, as shown by the writings of Muriel Spark.]

1726. Sale, Roger. "High Mass and Low Requiem. " Hud-
       son Review 19 (Spring 1966):124-34. [The Mandelbaum
       Gate]

1727. _____. "An Interview in New York with Walter
       Allen. " Studies in the Novel 3 (Winter 1971):405-29.
       Also in William H. Magee, Abstracts of English
       Studies 16 (January 1973):320. [Spark is characterized
       as one of the writers whose novels continue the comic
       tradition in English fiction and take comedy to be more
       serious than tragedy.]

1728. _____. "The Newness of the Novel. " Hudson Re-
       view 16 (Winter 1963-64):601-609. [The Girls of
       Slender Means]

1729. _____. "Novels, and Being a Novelist. " Hudson
       Review 15 (Spring 1962):134-42. [The Prime of Miss
       Jean Brodie]

1730. Schmidt, Sandra. "Memory's Loss--Novel's Gain?"
       Christian Science Monitor, 9 December 1965, p. 19.
       [The Mandelbaum Gate]

1731. Schneider, Harold W. "A Writer in Her Prime: The
       Fiction of Muriel Spark. " Critique: Studies in Modern
       Fiction 5 (Fall 1962):28-45. Also in Donald M. Mur-
       ray, Abstracts of English Studies 6 (May 1963):210.
       [The Bachelors, The Go-Away Bird, Memento Mori,
       The Prime of Miss Jean Brodie]

1732. Scrutton, Mary. "New Novels. " New Statesman and
       Nation 53 (23 Februrary 1957):253. [The Comforters]

1733. Sears, Sallie. "Too Many Voices." Partisan Review
      31 (Summer 1964):471, 473-75. [The Girls of Slender
      Means]

1734. Shrapnel, Norman. "An Anatomy of Violence." Man-
      chester Guardian, 4 March 1960, p. 8. [The Ballad
      of Peckham Rye]

1735. _____. "From Grave to Cradle." Manchester
      Guardian Weekly, 27 October 1960, p. 11. [The
      Bachelors]

1736. Simpson, N. F. "Second Sight." Time and Tide
      [London] 42 (29 June 1961):1077. [Voices at Play]

1737. Skorodenko, V. [Foreword to Russian translation of
      stories.] Moscow: Molodaya Gvardija, 1971, 39p.

1738. Smith, Dawn. "Slender." Canadian Forum 44 (Au-
      gust 1964):116. [The Girls of Slender Means]

1739. Smith, William James. "Bizarre Vision of the Com-
      monplace." Commonweal 73 (28 October 1960):130-31.
      [The Ballad of Peckham Rye]

1740. Sokolov, Raymond A. "Spark: Desperate State."
      Newsweek 76 (30 November 1970):95. [The Driver's
      Seat]

1741. Soule, George. "Must a Novelist Be an Artist?"
      Carleton Miscellany 5 (Spring 1964):92-98. Also in
      Donna Gerstenberger, Abstracts of English Studies 7
      (November 1964):472. [Spark's The Girls of Slender
      Means is compared with Mary McCarthy's The Group.]

1742. Spacks, Patricia Meyer. "New Novels: In the
      Dumps." Yale Review 64 (June 1975):588-90. [The
      Abbess of Crewe]

1743. Stade, George. "A Spark, An Amis, A Rhys." New
      York Times Book Review, 20 October 1974, pp. 4-5.
      [The Abbess of Crewe]

1744. _____. "A Whydunnit in Q-Sharp Major." New
      York Times Book Review, 27 September 1970, pp. 4-
      5, 54. [The Driver's Seat]

1745. Stanford, Derek. [A commentary on Muriel Spark

and her novels.]   In Contemporary Novelists, pp. 1160-
62.   Ed. by James Vinson.   New York: St. Martin's
Press, 1972.

1746. _____.   "The Early Days of Miss Muriel Spark:
Some Prime Recollections."   Critic [Chicago] 20
(April-May 1962):49-53.   Also in Robert Yackshaw,
Abstracts of English Studies 5 (October 1962):386.

1747. _____.   "Author and Critic."   Times Literary Supplement [London], 1 November 1963, p. 887.   [Stan-
ford's Letter to the Editor intended as a reply to
charges made against him by a reviewer of his book
Muriel Spark.]

1748. _____.   "The Work of Muriel Spark: An Essay on
Her Fictional Method."   Month 28 (August 1962):92-99.
Also in Douglas B. MacEachen, Abstracts of English
Studies 5 (November 1962):477.

1749. Sullivan, Richard.   "The Spark of Recognition."
Chicago Tribune Book World, 29 September 1968, p.
3.   [The Public Image]

1750. Sullivan, Walter.   "Updike, Spark and Others."
Sewanee Review 74 (Summer 1966):709, 713-15.   [The
Mandelbaum Gate]

1751. Swinden, Patrick.   "Plots."   In Patrick Swinden, Unofficial Selves: Character in the Novel from Dickens
to the Present Day, pp. 203-58.   New York: Harper
& Row, Publishers; Barnes & Noble Book, 1973.

1752. Sykes, Gerald.   "The Bewitching Ways of Dougal
Douglas."   New York Times Book Review, 28 August
1960, pp. 26-27.   [The Ballad of Peckham Rye]

1753. Tennant, Emma.   "Holy Joke."   Listener 92 (14 November 1974):649.   [The Abbess of Crewe]

1754. Thompson, Marjorie.   "Chapter XIV: The Nineteenth
Century and After, II."   In The Year's Work in Eng-
lish Studies, vol. 34 (1953), pp. 292-312.   Ed. by
Frederick S. Boas and Beatrice White.   London:
Geoffrey Cumberlege for Oxford University Press,
1955.   [On John Masefield, pp. 294-95.]

1755. Tindall, Gillian.   "Spark of Death."   New Statesman

80 (25 September 1970):387-88. [The Driver's Seat,
The Girls of Slender Means, Memento Mori, The
Prime of Miss Jean Brodie, The Public Image]

1756. Tracy, Honor. "The Richness of Muriel Spark."
New Republic 153 (9 October 1965):28-29. [The
Mandelbaum Gate]

1757. Tracy, Robert. "The Mandelbaum Gate." Southern
Review [Baton Rouge] 3 (April 1967):529-31.

1758. Treece, Henry. "What a Set!" Poetry Quarterly
[London] 13 (Winter 1951-52):188-89. [Child of Light]

1759. Trevor, William. "Discipline from Within." Manchester Guardian, 14 June 1968, p. 9. [The Public
Image]

1760. Trewin, J. C. "Peak and Valley." Illustrated London News, 13 October 1962, p. 572. [Review of the
New Arts Theatre performance of "Doctors of Philosophy."]

1761. Tuohy, Frank. "Rewards and Bogies." Spectator
207 (3 November 1961):634. [The Ballad of Peckham
Rye, Memento Mori, The Prime of Miss Jean Brodie]

1762. Updike, John. "Between a Wedding and a Funeral."
New Yorker 39 (14 September 1963):192-94. [The
Girls of Slender Means]

1763. _____. "Creatures of the Air." New Yorker 37
(30 September 1961):161-62, 166-67. [The Bachelors]

1764. _____. "Topnotch Witcheries." New Yorker 50 (6
January 1975):76-81. [The Abbess of Crewe]

1765. V., J. "Letters of Mary Shelley." San Francisco
Chronicle, 9 May 1954, p. 25. [My Best Mary]

1766. Vančura, Zdeněk. "Současné Britské Spisovatelky, I:
Muriel Sparková" ["Contemporary British Women
Novelists, I: Muriel Spark"]. Časopis Pro Moderni
Filologii [Prague] 52 (1970):1-9.

1767. Vonalt, Larry P. "Five Novels." Sewanee Review
73 (Spring 1965):333, 335-37. [Shirley Ann Grau,

The Keepers of the House; Marion Montgomery, Dar-
rell; Fred Chappell, It Is Time, Lord; Muriel Spark,
The Girls of Slender Means; Albert J. Guerard, The
Exiles]

1768.   Ward, Aileen.   "The Ways of the Brontës. "   Book
Week 4 (18 September 1966):5, 19. [Emily Brontë:
Her Life and Work]

1769.   Warnke, F. J.   "Some Recent Novels: A Variety of
Worlds. "   Yale Review 50 (June 1961):627, 632. [The
Bachelors]

1770.   Watts, Richard, Jr.   "Rise and Fall of Jean Brodie. "
New York Theatre Critics' Reviews 29 (week of 22
January 1968):383.   ["The Prime of Miss Jean Brodie"]

1771.   Waugh, Auberon.   "The Lost Leader. "   Spectator 219
(22 December 1967):783.   [Collected Poems I, Collected Stories I]

1772.   _____.   "A Novel to (of all things) Enjoy. "   National Review 15 (22 October 1963):359-60. [The Girls of
Slender Means]

1773.   _____.   "Spark Plug. "   Spectator 230 (17 March
1973):331-32. [The Hothouse by the East River]

1774.   Waugh, Evelyn.   "Love, Loyalty, and Little Girls. "
Cosmopolitan 157 (February 1962):38. [The Prime of
Miss Jean Brodie]

1775.   _____.   "Something Fresh. "   Spectator 198 (22
February 1957):256. [The Comforters]

1776.   _____.   "Threatened Genius: Difficult Saint. "
Spectator 207 (7 July 1961):28-29. [Voices at Play]

1777.   Weatherby, W. J.   "My Conversion. "   Twentieth
Century 170 (Autumn 1961):58-63. [Remarks by
Weatherby, p. 58.]

1778.   Webb, W. L.   "Autumn Harvest of Short Stories. "
Manchester Guardian, 28 November 1958, p. 8. [The
Go-Away Bird]

1779.   Weeks, Edward.   "The Beehive. "   Atlantic Monthly

184   Muriel Spark

212 (October 1963):148. [The Girls of Slender Means]

1780. Weisberg, Edzia. "Fiction Chronicle. " Partisan Review 5-6 (1961):716-22. [The Bachelors]

1781. Welcher, Jeanne K. "Muriel Spark: Five Joyful Mysteries. " Catholic Book Reporter 1 (November-December 1961):6-7.

1782. White, Beatrice. "Chapter XIII: The Nineteenth Century and After, I. " In The Year's Work in English Studies, vol. 31 (1950), pp. 222-45. Ed. by Frederick S. Boas and Beatrice White. London: Geoffrey Cumberlege for Oxford University Press, 1952. [On Tribute to Wordsworth, p. 222.]

1783. Whitehorn, Katharine. "Three Women. " Encounter 21 (December 1963):78, 80-82. [Mary McCarthy, Muriel Spark, and Iris Murdoch]

1784. Wildman, John Hazard. "Translated by Muriel Spark. " In Nine Essays in Modern Literature, pp. 129-44. Ed. by Donald E. Stanford. Baton Rouge, La.: Louisiana State University Press, 1965. [Reviewed in Choice 2 (1965):382.]

1785. Wilkie, Brian. "Muriel Spark: From Comedy to Disaster and Grace. " Commonweal 79 (11 October 1963):80-81. [The Girls of Slender Means]

1786. Wilson, Angus. "Journey to Jerusalem. " Observer Weekend Review [London], 17 October 1965, p. 28. [The Mandelbaum Gate]

1787. Wolfe, Peter. "Choosing the Death. " New Republic 163 (3 October 1970):27. [The Driver's Seat]

1788. Wood, Michael. "Fiction in Extremis. " New York Review of Books 21 (28 November 1974):29. [The Abbess of Crewe]

1789. Worthy, Judith. "On Sparkles. " Books and Bookmen 11 (December 1965):40. [The Mandelbaum Gate]

1790. Yglesias, Helen. "Going to Jerusalem. " Nation 201 (22 November 1965):392-94. [The Mandelbaum Gate]

D. MOTION PICTURES

1791. "The Driver's Seat." A Francesco Rossellini production, starring Elizabeth Taylor. Filmed in 1975.

1792. "The Prime of Miss Jean Brodie." Synopsis and critique published in Filmfacts: A Publication of the American Film Institute [ed. by Ernest Parmentier] 12, no. 2 (1969):25-27. A 20th Century-Fox Picture. Producer: Robert Fryer; Co-Producer: James Cresson. Director: Ronald Neame. Screenplay: Jay Presson Allen, based on her play which was adapted from the novel The Prime of Miss Jean Brodie, by Muriel Spark. Photography: Ted Moore. Editor: Norman Savage. Production Designer: John Howell. Art Direction: Brian Herbert. Music composed by Rod McKuen, arranged and conducted by Arthur Greenslade. Sound: Jock May, Gordon McCallum, and Winston Ryder. Costumes: Elizabeth Haffenden and Joan Bridge. Makeup: Ernie Gasser. Production Supervisor: David Anderson. Assistant Director: Ted Sturgis. Location scenes filmed in London and Edinburgh, interiors at Pinewood Studios (London). Color by DeLuxe. Length: 116 minutes. Cast: Jean Brodie--Maggie Smith; Teddy Lloyd--Robert Stephens; Sandy--Pamela Franklin; Gordon Lowther--Gordon Jackson; Miss MacKay--Celia Johnson; Mary McGregor --Jane Carr; Jenny--Diane Grayson; Monica--Shirley Steedman; Miss Campbell--Margo Cunningham; Miss Gaunt--Ann Way; Miss Mackenzie--Isla Cameron; Miss Kerr--Helena Gloag; Miss Alison Kerr--Molly Weir; Emily Carstairs--Lavina Lang; Miss Lockhart--Rona Anderson; Mr. Burrage--John Dunbar. Schoolgirls are: Kristen Hatfield, Hilary Berlin, Jennifer Irvine, Gillian Evans, Janette Sattler, Diane Robillard, Helen Wigglesworth, Antonia Moss, Antoinette Biggerstaff.

Reviews of "The Prime of Miss Jean Brodie"

1793. Anonymous. Punch 256 (2 April 1969):vii.

1794. Kauffman, Stanley. New Republic 160 (1 March
       1969):20.

1795. Wolf, William. Cue: Magazine for New York
       and Suburbs 38 (8 March 1969):72.

E. INTERVIEWS

1796. Anonymous. [Title unknown.] Observer Colour Magazine [London], 7 November 1971, pp. 73-74. [An interview with reference to Spark's deployment of "aggressively surreal tactics," as in The Hothouse by the East River.]

1797. _____. "Edinburgh's Muriel Spark Hides in South." The Scotsman, 20 August 1962, p. 4. [An interview with reference to The Prime of Miss Jean Brodie.]

1798. _____. "Interview with Muriel Spark." Observer Colour Magazine [London], 17 October 1965 [pages unknown]

1799. _____. "The Prime of Muriel Spark." Observer Colour Magazine [London], 17 October 1965, p. 10. [An interview with reference to The Mandelbaum Gate.]

1800. Gillhan, Ian. "Keeping It Short--Muriel Spark Talks about her Books to Ian Gillhan." Listener 84 (1970): 411-13.

1801. Howard, Elizabeth Jane. "Writers in the Tense Present." Queen, the Lady's Newspaper and Court Chronicle [London] Centenary Issue (August 1961):135-46. [An interview with Muriel Spark, et al.]

1802. Kermode, Frank. "The House of Fiction: Interviews with Seven English Novelists." Partisan Review 30 (Spring 1963):61-82. Also in Barbara A. Paulson, Abstracts of English Studies 7 (February 1964):82. [Kermode discusses with Spark the relationship between fiction and reality.]

F.   BIOGRAPHIES

1803.   Anonymous.   The Author's and Writer's Who's Who.
[No editor given.]   London: Burke's Peerage Ltd.,
1963, p. 454 and 1971, p. 743.

1804.   _____.   The Author's and Writer's Who's Who.   Ed.
by L. G. Pine.   New York: Hafner Publishing Company, 4th ed., 1960, p. 364.

1805.   _____.   Contemporary Authors.   Vols. 7-8.   Ed.
by James M. Ethridge.   Detroit: Gale Research Company, 1963, p. 534.

1806.   _____.   Contemporary Poets of the English Language.   Ed. by Rosalie Murphy and James Vinson.
Chicago and London: St. James Press, Ltd., 1970,
p. 1035.

1807.   _____.   Dictionary of International Biography 1973.
Part II.   General ed.:   Georgina A. Reynolds.   Cam-
bridge, London, and Dartmouth, England: Melrose
Press Ltd., 1972, p. 1225.

1808.   _____.   The International Who's Who 1964-65, The
International Who's Who 1965-66, The International
Who's Who 1966-67, The International Who's Who 1967-
68, The International Who's Who 1968-69, The International Who's Who 1969-70, The International Who's
Who 1970-71, The International Who's Who 1971-72,
The International Who's Who 1972-73.   The International Who's Who 1973-74, The International Who's
Who 1974-75.   [No editor given.]   London: Europa
Publications Ltd., 1964, p. 1025; 1965, p. 1075; 1966,
p. 1154; 1967, p. 1229; 1968, pp. 1246-47; 1969,
p. 1407, 1970, p. 1514; 1971, p. 1549; 1972, p. 1579;
1973, p. 1599; 1974, pp. 1640-41.

1809.   _____.   The International Who's Who in Poetry.

Vol. 2. Ed. by Geoffrey Handley-Taylor. London:
Cranbrook Tower Press, 1958, p. 138.

1810. _____. International Who's Who in Poetry, 3rd
ed., 1972-73. Ed. by Ernest Kay. London and Dartmouth, England: International Who's Who in Poetry,
1972, p. 396.

1811. _____. 200 Contemporary Authors. Ed. by Barbara Harte and Carolyn Riley. Detroit: Gale Research Co., Book Tower, 1969, pp. 262-63. [Biog-
raphy and critical analysis of Muriel Spark.]

1812. _____. Who's Who 1961. [No editor given.] London: Adam & Charles Black, 1961, p. 2855.

1813. _____. Who's Who 1962, Who's Who 1963, Who's
Who 1964, Who's Who 1965, Who's Who 1966. [No
editor given.] London: Adam & Charles Black and
New York: St. Martin's Press, 1962, p. 2872; 1963,
pp. 2862-63; 1964, p. 2859; 1965, p. 2874; 1966, p.
2872.

1814. _____. Who's Who 1967-1968, Who's Who 1968-
1969, Who's Who 1969-1970, Who's Who 1970-1971,
Who's Who 1971-1972, Who's Who 1972-1973, Who's
Who 1973-1974, Who's Who 1974-1975. [No editor
given.] New York: St. Martin's Press, 1967, p.
2871; 1968, p. 2877; 1969, pp. 2901-2902; 1970, p.
2920; 1971, pp. 2957-58; 1972, pp. 2996-97; 1973,
p. 3034; 1974, p. 3073.

1815. _____. Who's Who 1975. [No editor given.] London: Adam & Charles Black Ltd., 1975, p. 2959.

1816. _____. Who's Who in the World 1971-1972, Who's
Who in the World 1974-1975. [No editor given.] Chicago: Marquis Who's Who, Inc., 1st ed., 1970, p.
858; 2nd ed., 1973, p. 939.

1817. _____. The Writers Directory 1971-73. Ed. by
A. G. Seaton. Chicago and London: St. James Press,
1971, p. 422.

1818. _____. The Writers Directory 1974-76. [No editor
given.] London: St. James Press and New York: St.
Martin's Press, 1973, pp. 763-64.

1819.   Hynes, Samuel. "In the Great Tradition: The Prime
        of Muriel Spark. " Commonweal 75 (23 February
        1962):562-63.

1820.   Long, Shirley. "Muriel Spark: Success, but Still
        the Attic. " World Digest [London] 45 (July 1961):
        88-89.

1821.   Osborne, Charles. "Spark, Muriel (1918-   ). " In
        The Penguin Companion to English Literature, p. 490.
        Ed. by David Daiches.   New York: McGraw Hill
        Book Company, 1971.

1822.   Richardson, Kenneth Ridley. "Spark, Muriel (1918-
). " In Twentieth Century Writing: A Reader's
        Guide to Contemporary Literature, pp. 577-78.   Ed.
        by Kenneth R. Richardson.   Levittown, N. Y. : Trans-
        atlantic Arts, Inc. , 1971.

1823.   Stanford, Derek. "Muriel (Sarah) Spark. " In Con-
        temporary Novelists, pp. 1159-62.   Ed. by James
        Vinson.   Preface by Walter Allen.   London: St.
        James Press, Ltd. , and New York: St. Martin's
        Press, 1972.

G. BIBLIOGRAPHIES

1824. Anonymous. "Publications [of Muriel Spark]. " In
Contemporary Poets of the English Language, pp.
1035-36. Ed. by Rosalie Murphy and James Vinson.
Chicago and London: St. James Press, Ltd. , 1970.

1825. Adelman, Irving, and Dworkin, Rita. "[Bibliography
of] Muriel Spark, 1918- . " In Irving Adelman and
Rita Dworkin, The Contemporary Novel: A Checklist
of Critical Literature on the British and American
Novel Since 1945, pp. 477-81. Metuchen, N.J.: The
Scarecrow Press, Inc. , 1972.

1826. Aitken, W. R. In Cassell's Encyclopedia of World
Literature, vol. 3, p. 547. Ed. by S. H. Steinberg.
New York: William Morrow & Company, Inc. , 1973.

1827. Bryer, Jackson R. , and Magee, Nanneska N. "The
Modern Catholic Novel: A Selected Checklist of Criti-
cism. " In The Vision Obscured, pp. 241-68. Ed. by
Melvin J. Friedman. New York: Fordham University
Press, 1970. [On Muriel Spark, pp. 253-55.]

1828. Leverenz, Vergene F. "Muriel Camberg Spark. " In
Encyclopedia of World Literature in the 20th Century,
pp. 343-44. Ed. by Wolfgang Bernard Fleischmann.
New York: Frederick Ungar Publishing Co. , 1971.

1829. Malkoff, Karl. Muriel Spark. New York and London:
Columbia University Press, 1968, pp. 47-48. [Short
bibliography on Spark.]

1830. Mannheimer, Monica. Pilot Book to Muriel Spark,
The Go-Away Bird and Other Stories: Introduction
and Commentary. Stockholm: Almqvist & Wiksell,
1971 [pages of brief English bibliography unknown].

1831. Mellown, Elgin W. "Spark, Muriel Sarah (1918-   ). "

In A Descriptive Catalogue of the Bibliographies of
20th Century British Writers, p. 354. Comp. by Elgin W. Mellown.   Troy, N.Y.: Whitston Publishing
Co., 1972. [Brief checklist of some bibliographic
references.]

1832. Palmer, Helen H., and Dyson, Ann Jane, comps.
        English Novel Explication: Criticisms to 1972.   Ham-
        den, Conn.: The Shoe String Press, Inc., 1973, pp.
        241-42. [On some of Spark's novels.]

1833. Stanford, Derek.   "Muriel (Sarah) Spark." In Con-
        temporary Novelists, pp. 1159-62.   Ed. by James
        Vinson.   Preface by Walter Allen.   London: St.
        James Press, Ltd. and New York: St. Martin's
        Press, 1972.

1834. Stone, Bernard.   "Bibliography [of Muriel Spark]." In
        Derek Stanford, Muriel Spark: A Biographical and
        Critical Study, pp. 167-84.   Fontwell, Sussex and Lon-
        don: Centaur Press, Ltd., 1963.

1835. Stubbs, Patricia.   "Muriel Spark: A Select Bibliog-
        raphy." In Patricia Stubbs, Muriel Spark, pp. 34-35.
        Harlow, Essex, England: Longman Group Ltd., 1973.

1836. Temple, Ruth Z., and Tucker, Martin, eds.   Twen-
        tieth Century British Literature: A Reference Guide
        and Bibliography.   New York: Frederick Ungar Pub-
        lishing Co., 1968, p. 102. [Brief checklist of studies
        done on Spark and her novels.]

1837. Walker, Warren S., comp.   Twentieth-Century Short
        Story Explication: Supplement I to Second Edition,
        1967-1969.   Hamden, Conn.: The Shoe String Press,
        Inc., 1970, p. 228. [On some of Spark's short sto-
        ries.]

INDEX OF AUTHORS

Aaron, D. 114
Abelló, M. 304
Ackroyd, P. 532-33, 1508
Adams, P. 957, 974, 1021,
1060, 1118, 1140
Adams, R. 159
Adelman, I. 932, 1825
Adler, R. 1509
Ahlin, L. 534
Aitken, W. 920, 1836
Albérès, R. 535
Aleu, J. 104, 216
Allen, B. 958, 1510
Allen, J. 1126, 1215
Allen, W. 429-31, 536-37,
1511-12
Allott, M. 538
Allsop, K. 432
Amis, K. 309, 686
Amis, M. 539-40
Anderson, T. 472
Andreini, G. 74, 134, 147,
176, 271
Annan, G. 55, 1443, 1513
Anthony, M. 489
Armour, R. 1514
Arnaud, P. 541
Ashdown, E. 473
Avant, J. 6, 56, 98, 211,
1022

Bacon, M. 1515
Bailey, P. 542
Baker, R. 921, 933
Balakian, N. 543
Baldanza, F. 433, 439, 471,
544-46, 934, 1516
Balliett, W. 351, 1517
Bannon, B. 36, 160, 959,

1061, 1109, 1163, 1374
Barasch, F. 646
Barnes, C. 405, 1216-18,
1518
Baro, G. 1519
Barrett, W. 137, 547-48
Barrows, J. 549, 895, 922
Bart, I. 1158
Batchelor, B. 550
Bedford, S. 1520-21
Bell, P. 551
Bellasis, M. 1522
Benét, W. 909
Bentley, P. 1523
Berek, P. 161
Bergonzi, B. 434, 552, 1432
Beriger, H. 553
Berthoff, W. 435, 554-55,
1433, 1524
Betjeman, J. 556
Betsky, C. 212
Betts, D. 1083
Billington, M. 557
Bin, N. 69
Birstein, A. 1525
Blackburn, S. 80
Blackburn, T. 1526
Blair, H. 558
Blehl, V. 1439
Blondell, J. 1327, 1414
Bloom, E. 1527-28
Boas, F. 1536, 1782
Boegel, J. 1141
Boira, J. 1096
Boisen, M. 1072
Borklund, E. 923
Bosch, A. 146, 1013, 1038
Bostock, A. 115
Bottorff, W. 1676

193

Index of Authors

INDEX OF TITLES

"Conundrum" 1231
Conviction 363
"The 'Creative Waywardness' of Iris Murdoch" 795
"Creatures of the Air" 1763
"Criminals at Large" 1529
"Criticism, Effect and Morals" 1357
"Criticism of Iris Murdoch: A Selected Checklist" 936
"Crossing-Point" 1567
Current Biography Yearbook 906
"The Curtain Blown by the Breeze" 1282
Czas Aniołów 267

"Daisy Overend" 1283
"The Dancers" 1232
Dans le Filet 296
"The Dark Glasses" 1284
"The Darkening Vision of Muriel Spark" 1719
"The Darkness of Practical Reason" 424
"Day of Rest" 1233
"De lo Espeluznante a la Alegoria" 1684
"The Death of Fiction" 1725
"The Deceptions of Muriel Spark" 1658
"Deep Mist and Shallow Water" 494
Une Défaite Assez Honorable 93
Degrees of Freedom: The Novels of Iris Murdoch 439
"Delight and Instruction" 691
Les Demi-Justes 148
Les Demoiselles de Petite Fortune 1032
"Demonology and Dualism: The Supernatural in Issac Singer
    and Muriel Spark" 1659
"The Desegregation of Art" 1182
"A Devil Called Douglas" 1470
"A Devil-Figure in a Contemporary Setting: Muriel Spark's
    The Ballad of Peckham Rye" 1555
"The Devil's at Work Around the Clock" 1687
A Descriptive Catalogue of the Bibliographies of 20th Century
    British Writers 939
"The Devious Involutions of Human Character and Emotions:
    Reflections on Some Recent British Novels" 726
Devojka Italijanka 125
"Dialogue as Trenchant as a 5-to-1 Martini" 620
Dictionary of International Biography 1807
"The Difficulties of Commitment: Some Recent Novels" 1699
"The Dilemmas of Language: Sartre's La Nausée and Iris
    Murdoch's Under the Net" 868
"Dirty Words?" 598
"Discipline from Within 1759

INDEX OF SUBJECTS

233